History and Imagination

Reenactments for Elementary Social Studies

Ronald Vaughan Morris

ROWMAN & LITTLEFIELD EDUCATION
A division of

ROWMAN & LITTLEFIELD PUBLISHERS, INC.
Lanham • New York • Toronto • Plymouth, UK

KH

Published by Rowman & Littlefield Education
A division of Rowman & Littlefield Publishers, Inc.
A wholly owned subsidary of The Rowman & Littlefield Publishing Group, Inc.
4501 Forbes Boulevard, Suite 200, Lanham, Maryland 20706
http://www.rowmaneducation.com

Estover Road, Plymouth PL6 7PY, United Kingdom

British Library Cataloguing in Publication Information Available

Library of Congress Cataloging-in-Publication Data

Morris, Ronald V.
  History and imagination : reenactments for elementary social studies / Ronald Vaughan Morris.
       p. cm.
  Summary: "In History and Imagination, elementary school social studies teachers will learn how to help their students break down the walls of their schools, more personally engage with history, and define democratic citizenship. By collaborating together in meaningful investigations into the past and reenacting history, students will become experts who interpret their findings, teach their peers, and relate their experiences to those of older students, neighbors, parents, and grandparents. The byproduct of this collaborative, intergenerational learning is that schools become community learning centers, just like museums and libraries, where families can go together in order to find out more about the topics that interest them. There is an incredible value in the shared and lived experiences of reenacting the past, of meeting people from different places and times: an authority and reality that textbooks cannot rival. By engaging elementary social studies students in living history, whether in the classroom, after school, or in partnership with local historical institutions, teachers are guaranteed to impress upon the students a special, desired understanding of place and time" — Provided by publisher.
  ISBN 978-1-61048-297-4 (hardback) — ISBN 978-1-61048-298-1 (paper) — ISBN 978-1-61048-299-8 (electronic)
  1. Social sciences—Study and teaching (Elementary)—United States. 2. History—Study and teaching (Elementary)—United States. 3. Historical reenactments—United States. I. Title.
  LB1584.M78 2012
  372.89′044—dc23   2011047090

♾ ™ The paper used in this publication meets the minimum requirements of American National Standard for Information Sciences—Permanence of Paper for Printed Library Materials, ANSI/NISO Z39.48-1992. Printed in the United States of America

11/26/12

In memory of Roy and Jeanette Polacek Morris
and Ralph and Berneice Hanna Vaughan

Contents

Acknowledgments   vii

1   Historical Reenactment for Children   1

2   How Teachers Can Conduct Historical Reenactments
in Their Own Schools   11

3   Contrasting the French with the British in North America:
Establishing Community within a Fifth-Grade Historical
Reenactment   23

4   Pioneer Diversity and Dissenters' Day   39

5   Community Celebrations and History Participation   57

6   Learning from a Community Festival or Reenactment   69

7   Historical Reenactment at a Living History Site   83

8   Extracurricular Social Studies at the Conner Prairie
Interpretive Park   109

9   Huddleston Farmhouse 1860 Victorian Life Day Camp   123

10   Integrating Music and Social Studies in an Extracurricular
Activity: The Voyageur Ancient Fife and Drum Corps   137

11   Conclusions   149

About the Author   157

Acknowledgments

I would like to thank the following people and institutions who have contributed to the success of this manuscript. Martha Morris, ever faithful and untiring, read, reviewed, and commented on the manuscript. I would like to thank my peers: M. Gail Hickey, Tom Kelleher, Karen Kimball for their interest, time, and comments about this project. I would like to thank Robert G. Williams for doing the photography. I would like to thank Teresa Downs for the Civil War period clothing for the cover art. I would like to thank the following students for appearing in the cover art: Katherine, Peyton, Shelby, and Tim.

The personnel at these organizations and sites willingly took time to explain their programs and let me write about their events. I would like to thank the personnel at the Indiana Landmarks Huddleston Farmhouse, especially Tina Conner. The articulate Wayne Goodman provided assistance with the Huddleston Farmhouse, and the gracious Jim Orr provided assistance with the Civil War Camp. I would like to thank the Huddleston Farmhouse personnel for permission to use the Farmhouse for the cover art location. I would like to thank my friend of many years, Leslie Martin Conwell at the Tippecanoe County Historical Association Fort Ouiatenon. I would like to thank Tim Crumrin, Sarah Morin, and the always helpful Nancy Stark of Conner Prairie for their assistance with this project. I would like to extend my thanks to the members and leaders of the Voyageur Ancient Fife and Drum Corps.

I would like to thank the publisher of *Childhood Education* for permission to reprint an earlier draft of the manuscript published as: Ronald V. Morris, "How Teachers Can Conduct Historical Reenactment in Their

Own Schools," *Childhood Education* 77, 4 (2001): 196–203. Reprinted by permission of Ronald V. Morris and the Association for Childhood Education International, 17904 Georgia Avenue, Suite 215, Olney, Maryland; Copyright 2001 by the Association. I would like to thank the publisher of *The International Journal of Social Education* for permission to reprint an earlier draft of the manuscript published as: Ronald V. Morris, "Extracurricular Social Studies at the Conner Prairie Interpretive Park," *The International Journal of Social Education* 23, 2 (2008–2009) and Ronald V. Morris, "Learning from a Community Festival or Reenactment," *The International Journal of Social Education* 23, 2 (2008–2009). In chapter 6, the Tippecanoe County Historical Association provided figure 6.1 as well as tables 6.1, 6.2, 6.3, 6.4, 6.5, 6.6, and 6.7; all are used by permission.

1

Historical Reenactment
for Children

The students were eagerly anticipating the annual trip to the old fort. The weekend trip consists of a full day of seeing historic sites before the students spend the night at the old fort and the next day seeing more sites. Students have always found the old fort to be a highlight of the trip. They tour the fort, have the grounds to themselves, perform guard duty all night, and cook breakfast over a fire the next morning. When I got the phone call a week prior to the event, I knew something had gone horribly wrong. The frantic voice spat out phrases and key words, "Horrible mistake . . . double booked . . . no space in the fort . . . terribly sorry . . . we don't know how it happened."

Now it was my turn to be frantic. I had a busful of fifth-grade students expecting a field trip. There was nowhere for them to stay. It was one week prior to the field trip. I had neither time nor budget to find something else. Quickly I countered, "Ask if we can bring our own tents and spend the night on the grounds outside the fort." It worked, and the staff at the fort was very gracious to work with. I had saved the field trip, but I knew that I was going to need to really sell this to the students to keep them from being disappointed.

When the students got to the fort, we set up our tents in the early autumn twilight before we walked over to get the tour. In the gathering darkness I could see something very strange. The double-booked group of reenactors in the fort had returned it to the way it was when it was a frontier outpost, and the scent of a hardwood fire was in the air.

Soldiers talked to the students to pass the time of day as they cleaned their weapons while horses strained at their tethers for the night and munched some hay. A camp follower cleaned the evening meal dishes away, brought out some mending, and comforted a small child while talking to the students about her experiences following the army. The students tiptoed past the officers' barracks and looked in, getting an understanding of how the enlisted men understood the social world of the officers;

*the officers had gathered around a table by the soft flicker of candle light to consume
an immense banquet and play cards. The students heard the scratch of a fiddle and
caught a bit of a lyric. In the cool evening mist it was a dream come to life; the
shadows haunted the fort and once again it was inhabited. The students were there,
the events seemed real, and I shall never forget the best accident that ever happened.*

WHY DOES REENACTMENT WORK FOR STUDENTS?

For many generations, when people gathered around dinner tables and
campfires they circulated historical narratives. Storytelling serves a
specific purpose in the fostering and understanding of the self; historical
reenactment takes storytelling a step further. Throughout history human
beings seem to feel compelled to reenact important dates from the past.
Thus, historical reenactment may become more of a quest for understanding and experiencing what people before them experienced during
important moments in history. There may be many reasons for this re-
playing of history.

One reason might be an attempt to find one's culture. Psychologically,
historical reenactors may experience increased confidence in their abilities to become an expert in certain areas. When explained from a social
perspective, group cohesion may be an important factor that links historical reenactors together in prosocial, commonly shared activities. Working
together for a common goal can be extremely rewarding to individuals.
Living historians celebrate both individually and together in preparation
for a historical-reenactment event, which sometimes occurs as much as a
year in advance.

History is a dynamic process. This indicates an active orientation of
learning, or a construction of knowledge by the learner. Children construct knowledge through language discourse with adults, but even more
so when paired with more-skilled peers. Psychologically and socially
speaking, students appear to derive increased confidence and self-esteem
from being respected and regarded highly among their peers. The group
camaraderie associated with supporting each other's learning through
investigating different time periods is likely to be rewarding on both an
intra- and interpersonal level.

The term "scaffolding" refers to the process of encouraging children
to actively construct their learning environments by letting them do the
work; in other words, not having adults doing for children what the
children can do for themselves. Furthermore, the adult or more-skilled
peer acts in the capacity of a facilitator and guides children when they
need assistance, and challenges them with more difficult work as needed.
Scaffolding is used as a formalized teaching technique in a classroom or
can be as simple as two or more children working on a puzzle together,

provided that one child is more skilled than the other one.

Scaffolding is an important and very rigorous teaching technique; it fosters children to strive to extend themselves beyond what they would normally attempt and challenges them to reach their limit without becoming too frustrated. The adult relinquishes control and assistance as soon as the child can work independently.

Children are likely to acquire deeper cognitive development and problem-solving abilities as well as a sense of trusting themselves to make correct choices and decisions as a result of being given a choice. Adults often scaffold each other in their own interactions because almost inevitably one adult becomes more skilled in one area than another. Thus, they may challenge each other and extend each other's abilities.

Historical reenactment is an important example of adults and children learning to see similarities in one another. For instance, historical reenactment consists of much more than costumes and accouterments; it involves scholarly study that entails many hours of examining and comparing different time periods. Often some practitioners of living history are people who are considered experts in a certain war or an area and act in the capacity of a mentor to other historians.

There is great potential that in many different situations there will be reenactors with quantitatively more experience than other reenactors. These specialists of living history are extremely knowledgeable in regarding their interests and are considered by others to be experts in authenticity. Many reenactors feel passionately about being as authentic as possible when reenacting. This appreciation and knowledge of material culture is deeply personal. Thus, it seems that historical reenactors seek out each other's advice on important matters such as authenticity, and they probably receive advice even when it is not solicited.

In historical-reenactment situations adults scaffold each other by working collaboratively to make sure that their information, as they understand it, is correct and as authentic as possible. Reenactors seem to be concerned with authenticity from the most obvious things such as setting, uniform, artillery, and furniture to the most minute things such as whether or not the militia wore eyeglasses from that time period or had clean-shaven faces in a particular battle.

Thus, reenactors' quest for authenticity places them in an expert–novice relationship in which they scaffold one another's learning, and while challenging each other's understanding of the topic, the expert helps the novice to deepen his or her understanding. The novice is not the only one to benefit from the expert–novice relationship. The expert must distill this insight to the most crucial elements. When children are immersed and interested in material, they are willing to open their minds and ready to investigate and construct their own meaning of events.

Teachers and educators of social education strive to interest students in social studies. For generations children have happily listened to such stories as "Robin Hood" and "Aesop's Fables" and played out gangsters or cowboys and Indians. What is it about social studies that sometimes extinguishes that inherent love of hearing stories? The answer might be that children feel too disconnected from the material; they may feel that it is someone else's history rather than theirs. Children must construct their own meaning of historical events rather than the events that adults perceive as being important for them to know. Whereas adults are primarily concerned with history being authentic, children must understand historical meaning from their own lenses.

When children are drawn to interesting stories or narratives and that interest is harnessed with action, children are much more likely to feel a personal investment in learning the material. Thus, assuming that the interest is there, the key is that social educators must harvest the child's inquiry. Historical reenactment may be the vehicle that allows children to become connected with history as they understand it.

If children are drawn to stories, then historical narratives can be very interesting to the young learner. Through identification with the material on a personal level, interest and learning cannot be far behind. Therefore, from the social educator's viewpoint historical narrative seems to be impactful in getting elementary students interested in social studies at a much earlier age than was originally thought.

When students work cooperatively with each other in a reenactment, they are socially prescribed to incorporate drama and play into the classroom context. Through communication with one another scaffolding is likely to be a part of the learning process. Different configurations of students work together with more-skilled peers and less-skilled peers, scaffolding each other in the classroom to achieve a common goal, which is to inquire, investigate, and prepare for a reenactment.

Through historical reenactment children learn from one another by sharing learning strategies and building on each other's ideas. It appears that deeper cognitive processes occur in adults and children through their encounters in peer interaction, cooperative work, and scaffolding through expert–novice relationships with each other. Furthermore, the engagement of children with social studies education through the medium of historical reenactments and dramatic play to foster cooperative learning will be addressed in terms of educational value and potential learning outcomes.

With regard to historical reenactment, scaffolding appears to occur in both adults and children alike. "Scaffolding" means to build, and when two or more persons share in the process, they are shaping and building on each other's thoughts, ideas, and constructions. Historical inquiry and interpretation foster scaffolding processes through discourse with one another. Historical narrative may at times foster differences in opinion about the interpretation of history; thus, the expert and the novice engage in discussion and deeper learning. Historical reenactment should be supported in social studies curriculums.

It appears that both children and adults engage with processes in the camaraderie and scaffolding that each group experiences. It also appears that historical reenactment is an effective strategy to fostering scaffolding processes in children and adults in terms of cognitive and psychosocial development. From a social studies curriculum standpoint, the contents of this book allow for investigation of the reenactment. The topic is warranted because historical reenactment seems to support scaffolding processes in the classroom, and because it is an activity that most children readily enjoy and respond to.

Historical reenactment invites children to be active participants in their learning, thus allowing them to feel as though history is personally meaningful to them. Also, reenactment gives them a deeper and richer context for social studies that they in turn can scaffold with peers. More importantly, the child who becomes interested and invested in history today through historical reenactments in elementary school may be the museum curator or living history expert in adulthood who scaffolds other novice adults and children alike.

DEFINITIONS

An open-air museum is a collection of buildings used to interpret a time, a theme, or a place. The interpretation may be of one place at different times, such as Old Sturbridge Village in Massachusetts, which with its collection of sixty thousand artifacts explain rural New England from 1790–1840, while their first-person program examines the 1830s. First person narrative refers to telling the story as "I" rather than in the third person referring to "they." The interpretation may be one time, such as at Plimouth Plantation, also in Massachusetts, which offers a mix of first and third person in 1620 on the *Mayflower II*, first person 1627 in the pilgrim village, and all third person c. 1627 in Hobomuck's homesite. The interpretation may be a theme, such as industrialism at Greenfield Village in Michigan. Conner Prairie Interpretive Park in Indiana is a nationally known living history or open-air museum that has acquired a national reputation in developing first-person historical interpretation.

Some sites, such as Conner Prairie Interpretive Park, provide first-person interpretation where, in addition to dressing in historic clothes the docents seem to inhabit the structures, perform their daily chores, and assume the role of a person from the time period by greeting visitors as if they lived in the past, too—"I just started making sausage"; the first-person interpreter engages the visitor in conversation as if they are both living in that time period. While seemingly very real the interpreter role plays a specific character from the past. Since the first-person interpreter may be representing life prior to the Civil War, they will not be able to answer some questions for the visitors, like "May I take your picture?"

Most docents interpret a site through the third person using a phrase such as, "They made sausage like this." A third-person interpreter speaks as a contemporary of the visitor, and they can answer all of the questions asked by the visitors. Most visitors have had prior experience with this type of interpretation, but the site content may seem more remote and unconnected when interpreters use this method.

RECREATING THE PAST

As nice as hands-on opportunities and period clothing are, social context and mindset are complicated factors and arguably speak more to histori-cal accuracy and understanding. Ultimately no one can recreate the past, especially the mindset of the people from a different time and place. Many aspects of material culture are also impossible to replicate. Just as it is difficult to enter the mindset of the people of the past it is difficult to leave the modern mindset.

Intrusions dominate the lives of students today, from the ubiquitous cell phone ring to the incoming text to the chime of arriving email. The pressure to immediately respond, respond, respond forces reflection from students' minds. The inclination to slow down and determine if the digital information being received is worth responding to is not the first impulse of students. Similarly, the crush of advertisements on T-shirts, computers, radio, busses, school scoreboards, TV, billboards, and grocery carts means that there is little time when a message is not being hurled at a student. A significant experience for students may be for teachers to offer them time away from ever-present electronics, and to give them the opportunity to live in a period of time responding more to the forces of nature than electronic jingles.

DRAWBACKS

There are serious drawbacks to using historical reenactment as an edu-cational method. It may be expensive to provide the materials and infra-structures need to provide this type of education, but, despite the cost, fourth-grade pioneer days are ubiquitous in the Midwest as is the Civil

War day in eighth grade. Even more costly is the relocation of historic structures to schoolyards, such as log cabins or one-room school houses, but many of these relocations occur and are maintained even in the face of budget shortfalls.

Historical reenactment does take time from the school day. Furthermore, it takes effort from teachers and community members to create these types of programs. The teacher could spend the same amount of time preparing many other types of lessons, and the community volunteers could spend their time removed from the public schools looking after their self-interests. The limited scope of the reenactment means that it does not speak for all people at all times in all places; it just post holes one particular topic by going in-depth at one particular spot. So, especially in the issue of curriculum standards and assessment through standardized testing, historical reenactment may limit the time a teacher uses in preparing for standardized exams, which loom quite large for classroom teachers in many states today.

Is reenacting learning through play? Yes. Teachers are always charged with exposing students to ideas and situations with new and different experiences that prepare them for living as a citizen in a democracy. Almost anything can be a learning experience by setting context, gathering information, and debriefing to follow up the events. Is it the most effective methods for specific goals and means? Obviously, many teachers think so and are doing reenactment in their elementary schools. What follows is a collection of case studies that illustrate what some teachers and cultural institutions have done to create historical reenactment for elementary students. Teachers are invited to see what has worked in the past and adopt ideas that might work with their students in their specific situations.

The case studies in this book provide insights as to how historical reenactment is used by elementary students in schools and in extracurricular experiences. Chapters 2 and 3 illustrate how teachers compare perspectives between two cultures through reenactment. Chapter 4 illustrates how teachers take the ubiquitous pioneer day and examine the multiple voices of dissenters.

While a common idea among museums and libraries, how educators work to include multiple generations in social studies learning activities hosted by schools is illustrated in chapter 5. Chapter 6 illustrates how a teacher takes another organization's event and helps students engage in decision making. Chapter 7 illustrates how a cultural institution creates outdoor-education programs for students. Chapter 8 illustrates how students participate in a long-term extracurricular program at a cultural institution. Chapter 9 illustrates how a differentiated curriculum supports feminist pedagogy through reenactment. Chapter 10 illustrates reenactment when music performance and not social studies is the main focus.

MILITARY REENACTING

Much of reenacting has a military or paramilitary flavor to it. Teachers need to consider the ethics involved in asking students to participate or how students are asked to participate in these situations. Many students are involved in middle-school Civil War days where they may be involved in a battle.

In one instance a group of fourth-, fifth-, and sixth-grade students had balloons tied to their ankles as they marched across a Civil War field. If one balloon popped they considered themselves wounded and if both popped they considered themselves killed. This bloodless battle ended with a great balloon stomp which, while great fun as a game, led to learning some very antisocial messages as to how much fun it was to wound or kill, the low cost of human life, and the lack of respect for life. Another group of students marched in formation emulating lines of a Civil War battle to a flurry of fireworks, which gives the audience the impression that war was more like a choreographed Fourth of July parade than carnage and suffering. Neither of these experiences is something to aspire to, and there may not be a good way for students to be involved in recreating a battle.

The students remember these lessons and teachers need to understand what they are teaching.

- Is this good for a society?
- How does this develop democratic citizens?
- What does it say about us as a culture that has repeatedly used its military since the end of World War II?

Multiple voices need to be encountered when working with military topics. Conscientious Objectors existed at that time, as did critics of war.

While there is much enthusiasm for military reenactment, social and political topics are just as interesting and help young students understand attitudes, values, and dispositions. Students compare ideas from the past to the present, and compare differing ideas from contemporaries.

PROCEDURAL NOTES

Multiple examples of historical reenactment exist for students around the world. I was particularly involved with students in fourth and fifth grades who received multiple opportunities for history and geography enrichment through historical reenactment. Editors of state and national publications noted the program in multiple articles. The students received the prestigious Certificate of Merit from the American Association of State and Local History for "offering a variety of programs for children" in 1984. Members of learned societies invited students to speak about the program at the Michigan Historical Society, Wayne State University, and across the Hoosier state.

Multiple examples of Indiana-based historical reenactments are included so that teachers may follow them when developing their own historical reenactments. I worked with some of these professionals in the classroom, and I have continued to work with them in qualitative research settings. These reenactments represent both the types of experiences teachers have access to and settings for naturalistic inquiry. Of course there are many other places in the country where teachers see excellent reenactment at work, but the examples selected are commonly the types of experiences teachers find or create for their students in North American communities.

A few items of organization are needed to help prepare for this event; historical clothing needs to be stored in individual bag labeled by size. This way the teacher can pass historical clothing out ahead of time, and the teacher immediately knows the size, and clothes do not become separated from students. Each student puts his or her clothes on his or her desk; they may change in the restroom.

Students need a helpful parent to help figure out buttons, suspenders, hooks, and which side is front on period clothing. Parents need to know where the safety pins are located for making quick alterations. At the end of the day students need to put all the clothes back in their bags neatly and ask parents to check for damage so that items can be repaired. A little bit of dirt was not a problem in historical times, but in the twenty-first century everything needs to be laundered between uses. Make sure that the clothing size is marked with permanent dye or a tag.

At this point the issues of subjectivity, selective accuracy, authenticity, and balance arise. Reenactors at museums are usually under strict guidelines on shaving, cleanliness, personal grooming, and the upkeep of their apparel. Reenactors may scare visitors with chewing tobacco, bad teeth, alcohol on their breath, smallpox scares, or the odors and stains of authentic laundry habits. Furthermore, livestock do not run through the streets of living history sites. Animal waste and garbage are contained. Modern guests expect modern facilities over privies. Most reenactors, including museum personnel, are widely selective about what they make allowances for, are careful about, and what they treat lightly. Many do fixate on material culture or just a few aspects of material culture, such as costume but not foodways.

Since the students may work around an open flame, they must wear cotton or wool and avoid synthetics for spark safety. Modern fabrics melt to the skin and natural fibers do not ignite with a loose spark; it probably is not a concern, but think about safety just in case. Fires should be in a pit, and one must never leave an open flame untended. Pits need to be filled with no trace of charcoal exposed at the end of the day; the fire site needs to be leveled and the sod returned to its original space. This precaution prevents someone from stepping in a hole after the fact and turning an ankle.

Arrange materials, tools, and ingredients for each group or activity in clearly labeled boxes; boxes are much superior to bags, because bags are difficult to mark, tend to tip, or can rip. This takes time up front, but on the morning of the event it saves lots of time and questions as people who are looking for ingredients or tools sort through a variety of materials. This organization serves as a double check to make sure all materials are accounted for. It is also a good way to make sure no group carries off more than they need of any one item, and people do not forget important items that they need for their group. Inform participants of the location of specialty items such as refrigerated goods.

For clean up, return all equipment, tools, and ingredients to a central location and proceed to a predetermined area for washing dishes. Outside areas are great for this activity, because then students do not need to clean up the clean-up area. Provide instruction for enthusiastic volunteers on cleaning unusual items. One group of great volunteers scrubbed all of that black stuff off a cast iron pot; the black stuff was the finished coating that made the cast iron pot nonstick and prevented rust. Check the restrooms before leaving the building and be prepared to vacuum unless the janitor is willing to help the group with this task.

Some final helpful thoughts:

- In case of rain, all of the activities move inside, so be prepared to assign spaces within the building: kindergarten room, teachers' lounge, teachers' work room, and the art room.
- Stick to a time schedule, especially for restroom breaks, otherwise students will disappear when it is time for the next set of instruction, requiring other students to wait for them.
- Store lunches in an easy-to-access spot.
- Locate a supply of firewood a month prior to the event. Make sure it is at the site ahead of time. Make sure it is a hardwood or from a deciduous tree. Hardwoods burn to coals, but pines just burn into ash.
- Clearly define areas that are closed to students and parents. Some people in the school will be very territorial of their particular spot even when they are not present.

2

✛

How Teachers Can Conduct Historical Reenactments in Their Own Schools

The flames spring up, igniting the tinder and sending out wood smoke; the eight-year-old students automatically move back from the cooking fire. When the coals are ready, a French marble cake will bake in a Dutch oven. A few feet away in the next group the shuttle slips between the threads before being pulled tight. Inch by inch, the garter tape grows until it is long enough to hold the stockings of a nine-year-old student in place.

These are just a few of the daily tasks undertaken by elementary-school students when experiencing a historical reenactment.

If you want us to like history . . . put visualizations and activities [into it] . . . don't keep it in the textbook . . . don't have it all reading and writing and . . . essays and tests . . . what you've got to do is . . take them out and show them how it was. How it was done. Let them do it themselves . . . active fun things to do make it exciting. —Nathaniel, a student reflecting on his reenactment experience

EDUCATIONAL REENACTMENT

A reenactment is the re-creation of a scene, time period, or event performed as authentically as possible by a group of people. When people attempt to go back in time through reenactment, they experience a culture that is alien to them. The people of the past are not only different with regard to attitudes and values but customs as well, which makes it very difficult for elementary students of the twenty-first century to interpret the lives of people from the past.

11

Students must construct their knowledge about the past by deconstructing their understandings of the present. This poses particular problems for social education in that students have limited understandings of the present and little understanding of the past, because of their limited number of experiences. To work backward from this limited understanding presents multiple opportunities for misconceptions.

An educational reenactment takes the in-depth cultural experience of participating in a reenactment and joins it with the educational structure of a social studies classroom. Students learn not only about events, but also about the people and the broader time period. The goal is to make the life of the student approximate life in a past time period as much as possible. In a reenactment students take on daily jobs and activities that are similar to what the people of that time had to do, primarily centered around making sure that they have food, fuel, shelter, and clothing. The students also must understand the conflicts, political issues, and community problems from the era.

Reenactments can be as varied as historical interpretation and imagination allow. Open-air museums such as Greenfield Village, Michigan, attempt to re-create a historic landscape, thus providing visitors a historic scenic context. Living-history farms such as the Lincoln Boyhood National Memorial in Indiana attempt to demonstrate how humans interact with the land.

At some historical sites, such as Colonial Williamsburg Foundation, families interact with the militia. Old Sturbridge Village in Massachusetts offers programs in which costumed students play the game of Graces on the village green. Conner Prairie offers a glimpse into a pioneer day through first-person historical presentations. Many Civil War sites reenact famous battles, including Perryville, Kentucky, and Gettysburg, Pennsylvania. Festivals such as the Feast of the Hunter's Moon at Fort Ouiatenon allow history clubs and student groups to visit, trade, and rub shoulders with the French, Native Americans, and English of the 1750s.

Many historic sites emphasize play over work, reflecting modern conditions over period reality of student work on the farm and in the home. Most sites readily make period toys and games available through their programing, but do not address how relatively rare toys and games were in early America compared to other forms of play and self-created toys. However, after playing these games on the grounds of a living-history site it is a pretty sure bet that when exiting the historic site the gift shop will be well supplied with these same items.

Although many family vacations have made reenactment sites their destination, and history clubs and gifted students have flirted with reenactments, there remains great untapped potential for use of historical reenactments as a way to teach social studies. This chapter, while providing general guidelines for doing reenactment, focuses on the French Colonial days. Of course, teachers may tailor these suggestions to suite their own classrooms and reflect the historical significance of their areas.

Reenactments can include a single class, a grade level, or the entire school. Teachers may be able to work with volunteers from a local historical site in creating reenactments. Many local historical societies are looking for this type of collaboration and are open to establishing a creative partnership with schools.

Collaborative programs such as these help the local museum to justify donations, get grants, maintain community support, and fulfill their vital educational mission. Students could perform guard duty around a historic fort, serve a Victorian tea in a house museum, or pump water on the grounds of a living history farm. Smaller museums and historical sites are often more receptive to innovation than are bigger sites that entertain large groups of children daily.

Working closer to home at a school outdoor-education lab or with a neighbor who has forested land can cut travel time. Reenactments do work quite well at school sites, which have the advantages of equipment, supplies, first aid, food, water, and rest rooms close at hand. The disadvantages include the incongruity of the twentieth-first century surroundings, which may take away from the intended experience. While a class does not need the attributes of a reconstructed or preserved pioneer village, farm, or fort for a reenactment, those facilities often do enhance the activity.

FRENCH COLONIAL REENACTMENT

The reenactment described here focuses on a twenty-year period of the French colonization in America (1741–1761). The French colonies of New France and Louisiana encompassed a large portion of North America—from the St. Lawrence River to the Great Lakes and to the Mississippi watershed. This time period in U.S. history is relatively unexplored by textbooks, making it ideal for reenactment. This article explains a teacher-planned reenactment that was carried out during the school day and offers guidelines for teachers wishing to hold their own reenactments.

When planning a reenactment, consider asking former students who are now in high school to serve as mentors; they can model ideas and activities from the time period. Once such reenactments have become a tradition, former students will remember when they were doing the activities and can help their younger charges to succeed. During the work sessions former students can demonstrate difficult tasks, such as working with wool. Such mentoring programs help provide important service learning connections and opportunities. Assign the mentors carefully, recognizing that some may be better at working with people, while others may be best at supporting services.

Parents are another great source of help during reenactments; ask them about their hobbies and interests. Some may be reenactors themselves or may have friends who pursue the hobby. Parents and school staff members may have applicable skills such as weaving baskets, storytelling, cooking, building a fire, sewing, singing, or gardening. Some may know folk songs or dances. Local historical societies are a great source of knowledgeable adults.

Provide a verbal description of the reenactment two weeks before the reenactment, and send written copies home with the student to facilitate their familiarization with the idea and the time period. The teacher should refer to this story periodically and review the information before the students begin the reenactment. Here is one example:

> In the year of our Lord 1751 the sun never sets on the realm of the House of Bourbon. Long live Louis King of France! Most of North American is part of either New France or Louisiana. You are a fur trader in training and have great dreams of becoming wealthy from the fur trade. Today you are on the banks of the Wabash River. You are taking time to learn your needed skills, meet people, and learn the way of the woods. It is hard work, but you still find some time for fun. You meet your friends—Indians that the Jesuits may or may not have converted. To reach this site you made the difficult canoe journey from Quebec by paddling up the St. Lawrence River, crossing Lac Ontario and Lac Erie, moving your canoe up the Maumee Portage at Miamis Town, and continuing down the Ouabache past Ouiatenon.

The reenactment setting will give the students an idea of important issues, international political situations, the place, and the time. The students determine what their roles will be in the reenactment, and they will get an idea of the people that they will portray and meet. Finally, they determine how they will be traveling in the wilderness and how the transportation system works in their time.

Reenactment experiences allow students to become immersed in a particular time and to learn what it would be like to live then as a common person. During the reenactment students not only labor as people did then, but participate in authentic games, dances, and amusements as well. The students work together as they explore the daily activities of the people through round-robin sessions. These activities give the students direct experience of life in a different time and hands-on involvement with a different culture.

For the French Colonial reenactment one group of students studied how to build a home in New France. The particular house they studied looks much like a European home—built by placing logs vertically on a log sill. The owner of the house trades in the French town of Vincennes. After completing the day's work scary stories were told in New France including the "Red Dwarf," "Devil Comes Courting," "Loup-garou," and "Fe'efile'."

Adults present information about clothing and the students model each item. The clothing illustrates regional differences, classes, and occupations; the clothing also demonstrates the extent of a worldwide trade network that reached to the fringes of this new civilization. Period clothing adds much to the whole endeavor. Clothing projects should be simple but authentic—moccasins, garter tape, sash, and bead necklace (see table 2.1).

First-person historical presentations, in which adult volunteers portray an individual or represent a group, serve as a general kind of presentation needed for all reenactments. The elementary-school students play the role of engaging the guests who are helping with the activities. Two key characters in the French Colonial reenactment were a priest and a voyageur (someone hired by a fur company to transport goods and workers between sites). They needed to build a lean-to shelter, dry their possessions, and repack their canoe for the rest of their journey.

The French Lady would talk about the journey to the new world and the world she left behind. She would describe how the community is growing, how it has changed, and how it is still on the edge of the wilderness. She could show the students her fine clothes from France and her work clothes; the Native American would give a brief demonstration of sign language and finger weaving. The French Marine shows the students how to load and fire the flintlock and how to make a fire with flint and steel. The French farmer could talk about his wooden shoes and village life. Each character starts with an article representative of his or her position in the colony and from there moves into narrative content that illustrates the story.

Avoid first-person presentations that are meant to represent famous people; few historical figures left enough documentation for us to know everything about their everyday lives. In addition, it is too difficult to stay in character. Avoid negative stereotypes and weak attempts at humor. Presentations are better if they are short and to the point. Always provide the opportunity for students to demonstrate or use part of what they have just learned.

BENEFITS TO THE LEARNER

Historical reenactments, as in role-playing activities, are flexible enough to reflect students' interest and to capitalize on local resources. Although

Table 2.1: Companies that Produce Artifacts for Historical Reenactments

Name	Annotation	Phone	Website
Artifact Company	Reproduction artifacts	888-965-0001	www.artifactcompany.com/artifactcompany/
C D Jarnagin and Company	French and Indian War to Civil War military uniforms and equipment	601-287-4977	www.jarnaginco.com/
The Culture Kit Company	Culture kits for classroom use	510-290-7504	theculturekitcompany.com/node/2
Flying Canoe Traders	Eighteenth-century clothing and gear	819-379-1755	www.flyingcanoetraders.com/
Heavy Metal Traders	Eighteenth- and nineteenth-century merchandise	815-786-2358	www.hmtraders.blogspot.com/
Historical Clothing Realm	Medieval	800-929-7035	www.historicalclothingrealm.com/
Irish Arms	Bronze Age to eighteenth century	353-49-8545856	www.irisharms.ie/
Jackdaw Publications	Primary source: documents and photographs	800-789-0022	www.jackdaw.com/
Golden Owl Publishing			
James Townsend and Son	Eighteenth-century clothing and gear	800-338-1665	jas-townsend.com/
Laidaker Historical Garments	Nineteenth-century clothing	717-538-9490	www.astitchintime.biz/index.html
LaPelleterie	Eighteenth- and nineteenth-century clothing		www.lapelleterie.com/
Lithic Casting Lab	Reproduction stone tools		www.lithiccastinglab.com/
Marquette Trading Company	Eighteenth-century clothing	309-251-1141	www.marquettetrading.com/shop/
Northwest Traders Inc.	Blankets	937-308-1591	www.nwtrader.com/
Old Sutler John	Uniforms, leather, tin, and tents	850-723-8047	www.oldsutlerjohn.net/
Panther Primitives	Tents	304-462-7718	www.pantherprimitives.com/
Personalizing the Past	Classroom artifact kits	415-388-9351	www.historykits.com/
Premier Designs Historic Clothing	Victorian to 1920s	800-427-0907	www.premierclothing.com/Extra/21-home-page/
Reconstructing History	Historical patterns	866-518-1558	www.reconstructinghistory.com/
The Smoke & Fire Company	Medieval, Scottish, Colonial equipment	800-766-5334	www.smoke-fire.com/
Windsong Traders	Mountain Men supplies	309.357.0356	windsongtraders.ecrater.com/
Wooden Hawk Trading Company	Mountain Men supplies	800-690-4295	www.woodenhawk.com/

no research has been conducted specifically on reenactment programs, many researchers have pointed to the benefits of dramatic experience, which shares some elements of reenactments.[1] Historical reenactments are valuable because they offer opportunities for students to synthesize information, role-play, discover what people value at a given point in time, and participate in re-created historical events.

Dramatic reenactments offer multiple ways for students to learn and organize content and skills. These benefits were given prominence in standards published by the National Council for the Social Studies and describe five key features of powerful social studies teaching: learning must be meaningful, integrative, value-based, challenging, and active.[2] Reenactments can incorporate all five of these elements.

STRATEGIES FOR REENACTMENT

The content of reenactments should be tied to the National Council for the Social Studies (NCSS) *Standards*.[3] Postreenactment discussion questions can be related to one or more of the standards (see table 2.2). By incorporating the NCSS standards in an educational reenactment, students do more than just experience what life in the past may have been like; they can examine content and relate issues. Reenactments must have definite goals with strong ties to academic objectives.

An ideal topic for a reenactment is an event that had a significant impact. You may want to select events that are part of local history, which gives you potentially greater access to people who are knowledgeable resources. Good topics will have documentation found in museums, archives, and libraries, but have had little or no previous interpretation. The material from museums, archives, and libraries provides the background information students use to develop their own interpretations through reenactment. As they do so, they will learn particularly useful strategies for illustrating conflict and cooperation between people, as well as demonstrating contrasting points of view.

As preparation the teacher may travel to historical sites, visit museums, and view professional reenactments. Local and state historical societies are helpful. In the case of New France, the available resources include the Tippecanoe County Historical Association, Fort Ouiatenon, Fort Niagara, Old French House, and Fort Michilimackinac. Other valuable assets include local high-school French teachers, university French professors, and reenactors. Next, the teacher should locate sources of accurate information for presenters to study and use, after which the students begin reading on the subject. A detailed plan may be submitted to the administrator.

Table 2.2: Student Research Questions Related to Social Studies Standards

Standard	Question	Accomplished
Culture	What identifies the people as French rather than English, Spanish, or Dutch?	Specifically examine the language, folk song, customs, folk tales, foods, fashion, and construction.
Time, Continuity, and Change	How has France influenced people?	All the first-person historical presentations examine this question.
Individuals, Groups, and Institutions	How do French colonists relate with the Native Americans?	Native American, Farmer, and Jesuit Priest first-person presentations examine this question.
People, Places, and Environments	How will French colonists survive?	Trading and Voyageur first-person presentations examine this standard.
Individual Development and Identity	What are the personal characteristics that describe the French traders and colonists?	The first-person historical presentations examine this standard.
Production, Distribution, and Consumption	How is trading done?	The first-person historical presentations presented by the Trader, French Lady, Native American, and Voyageur examine this standard.
Science, Technology, and Society	How do French Colonists and Traders use science and technology?	The Marine's gun and his flint and steel address this standard in a first-person historical presentation.
Global Connection	What connections remain with Europe?	The first-person historical presentations of the French Lady, Trader, and Marine discuss this standard.
Power, Authority, and Governance	What civil and military laws existed in New France?	The first-person historical presentations of the Marine, Priest, and Native American address this standard.
Civic Ideals and Practices	Who was considered a citizen of New France?	The first-person historical presentations of the Farmer, Voyageur, and French Lady examine this question.

To help offset some of the expenses associated with reenactments, teachers may want to apply for grants from the state humanities council, arts council, or a state department of education, to name a few possibilities. Contributions from families or gathered through a fundraiser are other solutions. Museum or local civic or historical groups also may be able to make donations.

Typically the students stay in small groups and rotate to all the different planned activities. The first group in a rotation always takes longer to get going; everyone will want to do everything. With practice the time periods will gradually grow shorter; if one is running short on time, cut the last session very short. For round-robin sessions fifteen minutes to fifty minutes is long enough for a good rotation at each section depending on the difficulty of the activities. Give the volunteers a two-minute warning to finish up the last few details.

Experienced and responsible upper-elementary students can assist small groups of younger children with activities. These students can be particularly helpful in monitoring the time schedule, leading younger students from place to place, and helping with crafts. Younger students should focus on answering the question, "How have things changed over time?" Many different activities can help students illustrate and explain their conclusions. The reenactment may also prompt further questions.

EVALUATIONS

The teacher needs to observe the event as it progresses; every portion of the experience requires evaluation throughout the day. Being ready to build on those interactions that occur naturally during the day is also important. A teacher should circulate during the reenactment, asking the students and volunteers for their opinions on how the day is going and reviewing what they have learned. The more notes that are taken and the more evaluations done, the easier next year's planning will be.

Because each student will experience the varied and complicated culture of the reenacted historic period differently, it becomes difficult to rely on traditional objectives and assessments. One possible assessment method is to offer guiding questions before the reenactment to help students focus their learning. First thing in the morning, ask the students to predict the answer and then talk with a friend about it; at the end of the day review the questions with the students. Have the students talk in groups of four and then discuss the answers with the whole group; on the day following the reenactment fill out a data-retrieval chart in class. Use a common set of questions to compare historical figures.

In a second assessment strategy, ask the students to write the story of their experiences during the reenactment. They should record their most salient observations in detail and compare that way of life to their present lives. Students should interpret the events and discuss why they were important. Through this process students may understand that some of their current concerns are not so different from those of people who lived in the past.

Other closing activities will help in evaluating the experience. Students may write a newspaper account for the local paper describing their adventures, or they could write a diary entry in the voice of a person from that time period. Still another possibility is for students to assume the role of a common person from that era and write a letter to a famous person of the time, asking questions about issues of the day. Students can make connections and comparisons from the past to the present on a wall chart comparing issues such as health, pollution, civil rights, and civic participation.

CONCLUSIONS AND STUDENT REACTIONS

Student reactions to reenactments are very favorable. As Aubrey, a student participating in the French Colonial reenactment stated, "We had a taste of what it was like for them." The environment students helped create surrounded them with experiences that stimulated their senses. The students got a better understanding of daily life through their experiences with the past. "We saw what it was like back then, saw what they went through, and [saw] what their daily hardships were like," said Jake.

By challenging students to immerse themselves in a different culture and time, striving to survive there, they learned to solve problems. Brent said, "You see things and then you end up doing stuff like the people used to do like building fires and cooking." Students integrated multiple skills and experiences into the event. "I remember chopping and splitting wood for the fire," confirmed Jordan. Reenactment, through hands-on experiences, can help students become more responsible for their own learning.

When teachers take the time to plan and conduct a reenactment, they bring students off the "sidelines" and into the heart of discussions and conversations. As Orion said, "You weren't viewing things; you were part of them." Students learned how people lived and related to one another. They also talked to one another about the events of the time, and they enacted these experiences. "The French Colonial reenactment was important because it helped us better understand how they lived. It made me understand that they had really hard lives, and it made us appreciate it [Colonial living] more," Laura explained. Reenactments offer time to explore depth of content, thus giving deeper meaning to issues and events.

NOTES

1. John Fines and Raymond Verrier, *The Drama of History: An Experiment in Co-operative Teaching* (London: New University Education, 1974); Paul Goalen and Lesley Hendy, "'It's Not Just Fun, It Works!' Developing Children's Historical Thinking through Drama," *The Curriculum Journal* 4, 3 (1993): 363–84; Elaine B. Kanas, "Echoes from the Classroom: Teacher Influence on Student Autonomy, Social Interaction and Creativity" (PhD diss., Columbia University Teachers College, 1994); Ronald V. Morris, "Common Threads: How to Translate Best Practices into Teaching," *Journal of Social Studies Research* 22, 2 (1998): 11–18; Phillip M. Taylor, "Our Adventure of Experiencing: Drama Structure and Action Research in a Grade Seven Social Studies Classroom" (PhD diss., New York University, 1992).

2. National Council for the Social Studies, "A Vision of Powerful Teaching and Learning in the Social Studies: Building Social Understanding and Civic Efficacy," *Social Education* 57 (1993): 213–23.

3. National Council for the Social Studies, *Expectations of Excellence: Curriculum Standards for Social Studies* (Washington, DC: National Council for the Social Studies, 1994).

3

Contrasting the French with the British in North America

Establishing Community within a Fifth-Grade Historical Reenactment

"The experience was great—I think this is better than doing it with a book, pencil, and paper because you actually get to feel what it was like back then."[1]

INTRODUCTION

In contrast to the French colonies of traders, the English colonies consisted of settlers. To highlight the differences between English and French colonies, their respective economies, geography, and politics need to be considered. The rivalry between these two world powers as they contested for dominance spanned centuries. Two very atypical Anglo Americans illustrate these ideas: one is George Mason and the other is Benjamin Franklin.

Some Americans such as Benjamin Franklin grew wealthy from their business in the colonies while others like George Mason were born into wealth. These Anglo Americans also illustrate the transatlantic world in which they lived. People, ideas, and trade frequently crossed the Atlantic Ocean along with mail, newspapers, and fashion. Living in British North America provided a better standard of living for most people than living in Europe.

To learn about British North America, fifth-grade students conduct historical reenactments for guests, parents, and the younger students from their school. The fifth-grade students use national, state, and local history to construct historical reenactments in the form of a living history day. The students use two months to research and present their characters, and they share the stories of the people. They talk about their props, costumes, and share their stories about how they came to their part of the community. The students use the school grounds for their staging area.

CREATING REENACTMENT

Students form groups of two or three including members of Parliament, members of the House of Lords, shipping insurance clerks, tax collectors, Virginia Anglican vestry members, the Adams family, New York slaves, Salem, Massachusetts boat captain and crew members, German Dunkers, and Delaware Native Americans (see table 3.1). The teacher, Mrs. M., does reenactment with her class because she wants her students' learning to be in-depth:

> I think that sometimes in the history books you have to cover so much that you have to leave out the interesting details. But when you can study one small time period in greater detail, then you get into really interesting things and personalities and interesting facts that you would otherwise have to skip over.[2]

Fifth-grade students in research groups use books, write scripts, practice, gather costumes and artifacts, and set up their area on the school grounds. Elementary-school students go from group to group in ten-minute rotations. Long-term research results in the fifth-grade students' development of full historical characters to portray within reenactment situations. They must apply their knowledge to remain authentic and in character. The more background information about people and events of the period the students have before entering the experience, the greater their potential for success.

In a finite school year of 180 days a teacher who takes time to do historical reenactment is able to justify the time allocation through the use of integrated curriculum where multiple objectives are covered through one activity. The amount of material covered may be diminished. During the progression of the reenactment the teacher spends significant time in learning skills required by the curriculum.

BRITAIN VERSUS FRANCE

Teachers used national standards for planning the events of the day to learn about Great Britain in comparison to France during the English colonial period (see table 3.2). Students learned about Culture, Time, Continuity and Change, and People, Places, and Environments from the

Table 3.1:   English Colonial Day Schedule

Time	Event	Activity
8:00	George Mason English lady	First-person presentation and slides First-person presentation
8:45	Student fashion show in historical clothing	
9:00	Rotation I (20 minutes)	A. Maps: England and the world B. Magic Square C. Chess D. Important people of the English world: Card game E. Atlantic trading: Simulation game
10:40	Restroom break	
10:50	French class	
11:10	*"What's the Big Idea?" Ben Franklin* by Jean Fritz	
11:30	Class II Rotation II (20 min.)	A. No constitution, Parliament, and the House of Lords B. Insurance and risk: Simulation C. What to tax? Simulation D. On the vestry: Simulation E. Rights timeline
12:00	Lunch	English cooking samples
12:30	Recess	
12:50	Rotation II (20 minutes continues)	
2:00	Debriefing	

Table 3.2:   English Colonial Day Story

You have been apprenticed to a wealthy merchant to act as his factor. You need to find out everything you can to understand the workings of the British Empire and especially its trade. You will have a variety of meetings with people who can tell you about British society and culture. You can talk to some people but others will be too far away so you will need to read about them. You will follow your master through business conversations and social episodes, where you will learn how he acts in public situations. By the end of the day you report what you have learned about British society and culture to your master.

standards of the National Council for the Social Studies.[3] Using these standards, the teachers created an experience where students learn about aspects of the English world and compare them to their previous experience with the French colonial period.

By knowing the standards, the teachers know what they will be assessing from their students. The students need to learn about the contest for empire that played across the North American continent. The students also need to know that the result of that contest eventually led to the independence of the colonies to form the new nation of the United States.

The English colonial day starts with a first-person presentation of George Mason, accompanied by PowerPoint slides, followed immediately by an English lady first-person presentation discussing her life in England and her opinion of the colonists. The point–counterpoint between George Mason and an English lady allows students to compare people on either side of the Atlantic and examine gender as a way to find out about the relations between people.

Students tell their peers about what they are wearing when they model period clothing, thus showing the differences in their clothing from the establishment of Jamestown, the initial English settlement to the American Revolution, and how social class determines what they wear. This explanation of clothing helps to define the span of time between Jamestown and Yorktown, the end of the American Revolution, which is difficult for students to comprehend. After these whole-group activities, students break into five small groups and rotate through learning centers where they encounter a variety of simulations to find out about life in colonial England.

The students may start with a collection of maps where they see the variety of colonies that belong to England and see how the maps change from the time of Jamestown to Yorktown. In addition to political and military history the students also work with social history. The students get a series of Magic Squares to find out what Benjamin Franklin did for fun. He really did create these to amuse himself; because he also played chess, the students get this opportunity also. Students learn about important people of the English-speaking world through a rummy type card game where they identify major accomplishments of English celebrities during the colonial era.

In their last rotation the students encounter a simulation game about Atlantic trading where students race to put together a cargo and move their ships through the triangle trade routes. The entire group comes together to learn some French vocabulary so they can negotiate with their enemies and then spend some time reading *"What's the Big Idea?" Ben Franklin* by Jean Fritz.[4] In a Venn diagram the students compare Ben Franklin with George Mason.

In the next set of learning centers the students encounter a government simulation illustrating the workings of Parliament and the House of Lords. The students have an opportunity to find out about insurance and a simulation of risk management in the shipping business. Next, as members of the King's ministry the student must decide through a simulation what they will do to raise revenue by creating a tax policy.

As members of the vestry they decide what work they will undertake through a simulation of the workings of an Anglican Church parish charged with the social services community needs in some colonies. Finally, they create a timeline of what rights and when each are earned in different colonies. The teacher works ahead of time with the school cooks to prepare a menu of traditional English recipes. The day ends with the students' debriefing to evaluate what they learned about life in the English colonies.

ASSESSMENT

Teachers assess historical reenactment when they compare the results of the program to the position statements of the NCSS. NCSS describes five key features of powerful social studies teaching and learning as being meaningful, integrative, value-based, challenging, and active.[5] Reenactment gives meaning to issues and events examined in great depth and gives students additional time to explore the breadth of content. The integrative reenactment suspends time for students and allows them to make decisions within the context of the event and surrounding situations through the power of drama.

The value-based reenactment encourages students to explore multiple perspectives and choose one of them. The reenactment is challenging in so far as the group must contribute to making physical and intellectual activities successful. The reenactment is active when the activity leads the students into becoming more responsible for their learning. Being meaningful, integrative, value-based, challenging, and active demonstrates the reenactment as a powerful method of teaching and learning social studies. To further understand the educational power of the reenactment requires examining a tool that unlocks culture.

FINDINGS IN EDUCATIONAL REENACTMENT: PARTICIPATING IN A HISTORICAL ETHNOGRAPHY

Students participated in reflection upon their experience in educational reenactment, and the student reflections are clustered into three groups: triumphs, problems, and solution generation. While breaking down the triumphs section of the reflection, students talked about several important aspects to their participation in the project. One of the thoughts where the students concurred was the power of the research over using a script provided by a teacher or a commercial product. "I like writing my own script because I learned more by doing all of the research than using someone's script."[6] Natalie clearly has engaged in the research process and found it to be meaningful in her learning, but other students found that the research stretched them beyond the limit of a defined part.

> You've got to know the information because if they interrupt you, you say a big word they don't understand they ask you what it is, you don't want to start all over again. So, you have to basically really learn the information other than the script.[7]

In addition to realizing that they had to work with the needs of their audience, they had to be able to respond flexibly and move beyond a set script. As the students reflected they realized this was a triumph because their research had made them experts on their topic. When students participated in historical reenactment, they had some of the same experiences found in ethnography.

Another area the students reflected upon and determined to be a triumph was the experiential nature of the experience. Through the reenactment format students used all of their senses to explore the topic.

> When we made the pemmican it helped me understand what it looked like, smelled like, and tasted like. I had also never seen . . . or touched a buffalo hide before. This also helped me understand the way they live better, such as the . . . clothes, cooking, tools, chiefs, and their horses.[8]

Students had new experiences that helped them to define concepts and imagine the type of life people would have lived. The students projected emotions and feelings onto the people in the past. "Well it just shows you how people were brave back then and you got to go to places and just feel what it was like."[9] Natalie found the reenactment experience very important to establish a connection with people and events of the past. She experienced events directly and determined an understanding of those events. Students found through the direct nature of the experience that they could draw parallels to their immediate lives and learn from enacting events.

The third area the students considered a triumph as they reflected upon their experience with historical reenactment was teaching and learning. This element of having ownership over knowledge was very important to the students who commented on it. Julie stated, "I think it's pretty neat because you get to tell people history and instead of . . . a teacher telling it to you, you get to tell somebody else."[10] She liked the communicative nature of the experience and sharing information.

Natalie also enjoyed the didactic nature of the experience while working with her peers. "I enjoyed acting everything out with my partner and teaching others everything we learned."[11] Students learn content and skills in situations where they engage in dramatic play by taking roles and interpreting characters. Students must examine both their action and their motives to describe what they did and why; students can study history early and use drama as a significant way to access and interpret information. Teachers and students must commit time to learn information in depth; students cannot learn knowledge without skills nor skills without knowledge.

The students identified two major problems: the age of the students and the adults who were supposed to be leading them. As to the age of the students, the students felt that they did not have the depth of knowledge to fully appreciate the reenactment. "The only thing that I think could have been better was the kids responding and interacting with the other people. There were several times when we asked question[s] they didn't respond."[12] While the students doing the reenactment responded to the lack of context of the students' experience, perhaps the preparation of the students was of more crucial importance.

The students doing the reenactment remained insistent about the developmental characteristics of their audience. "I think some of them were a little too young to really understand what we were talking about."[13] Some of this may have been their experience with their younger siblings or it may have been body language or movements of a less mature crowd that the older students noticed. The older students were not favorably impressed, but the older students did not have a formal way of assessing what the younger students took back to the classroom from the experience. The older students might have been more impressed if they had heard the debriefing conversations in the younger classrooms after the reenactments.

The other problem that the students engaged in the reenactment reported was the disengagement of the adults. This bothered the students a lot. "The parents/teachers wouldn't even keep the . . . [students] in line. In fact, the adult[s] were just as bad as the children. One of them was playing in the dirt!"[14] The students seemed to expect the adults, because of years of maturation, to behave like adults.

The students expected the adults to model on-task behavior for the younger members of the audience while not recognizing the time when they, the older students, did not offer these same listening skills to their teachers. "The teachers were worse than the kids usually."[15] The adults were in fact parent volunteers of the younger students. They received little preparation on what was expected of them in this situation. The older students who had worked hard to prepare for this experience expected the parents to take them seriously and to offer good listening skills.

The final cluster of responses illustrated solution generation through problem solving and reflection. One item that students worked with each other on was content knowledge and the development of their scripts.

"You need to know more than what is just in the script. Be prepared for questions."[16] The students understood the importance of visitor questions and possessing the flexibility to handle these questions.

The students also offered suggestions to create improved conditions for future years when they suggested that they would be able to take younger students through the experience next year as peer tutors. "Use the peer tutors to take the groups."[17] The students offered ideas about how they could improve the experience with specific recommendations. The students made specific recommendations when the class members were working with the teacher.

Mrs. M: So what grades do you think would be best?

Sean: Second and third. I think they would be a little bit more responsive and know what is going on.

Natalie: First.

Catherine: First through third.

Natalie: Kindergarten through third.

Sean: With the little kids they really did not understand what it was.[18]

It was important to the students who were involved in the reenactment to make sure that they had an audience that could comprehend the events and what was happening so appropriate interactions could occur. By communicating in back-and-forth exchanges between the students and the teacher, interaction provides a reflective loop of communication. Students engage in reflection in order to solve problems that emerge from their experience preparing for and then working with an audience.

A minority of the students who participated in this experience reported aberrant statements in addition to the main findings. The aberrant statements included information on interaction, and these are recorded as discrepant cases. John said, [We] "Should've done more interactions."[19] In addition, students talked about the interest to interact with more people through more opportunities. "I wish we could do it again for more people."[20] Some individuals wanted to do more with their presentation, or they wanted to expand their audience. Another individual wished to spend less time on research. "I thought the project was too long . . . I think that there should be less time to do research and more time spent on the settings."[21] The point of the project was for students to do research using multiple resources to gather information.

Even though the students on the whole reflected triumph, a discrepant case reflected a different view. "I have to question how much I really got out of it. If I read a book about it, I would know more."[22] This statement is puzzling due to the amount of time spent in researching the presentation, but perhaps the student felt that they should read more broadly rather than on a specific topic. While the students performed significant inquiry skills as demonstrated by the project, they did not see that their learning was significant. Individual students provide illustration of discrepant cases of showing divergent opinions held by reenactment participants.

REENACTMENT AS LIVED EXPERIENCE

When people attempt to go back in time through reenactment, they experience a culture that is both foreign and alien to them. The people of the past are not only different in attitudes and values but in health practices and customs as well. Through a reenactment program students experience life in a different time period; the reenactment program involves the participant in experiencing history. The students get to experience life as a common person; for a day they are an apprentice to the past. During the time period students participate in authentic games, dances, and amusements.

Whether one is visiting or participating, the reenactment offers instruction. Students produce products, ideas, beliefs, and they garnish a tremendous feeling of personal accomplishment when they finish their task satisfactorily. The students have a great deal of autonomy and responsibility for their learning through the reenactment.

In a reenactment the jobs and activities are similar to what the people of that time had to do; they had to make sure that they had food, fuel, shelter, and clothing. There is always something appropriate for everyone to do at all times; if the time period required guard duty, then the students also need to experience this task. The students need to participate in sustained contact with the symptoms of the society through activities, jobs, and diversions.

Work from times past has a different meaning; time truly requires invention and adaptation to solve problems. Discussing the event during and after the situation leads to insights for the people involved in the activities. In the reenactment format there is time for extra opportunities, exploration, and discovery. The knowledge students acquire helps them to produce a meaningful product physically, mentally, or emotionally. Students apply their knowledge to survive comfortably throughout the event, and the suspension of disbelief fosters the enactment of thinking as if the person lived in the historical event. This time in an historical event leads to discovering the pleasures and discomforts of that era along with time to think, listen, and question.

TEACHING AND LEARNING
THROUGH ETHNOGRAPHY AS METHOD

Ethnography endeavors to explore the culture of a group of people. Specifically within a culture ethnography probes the function of the culture, transmission of culture from person to person, nature of the culture, and emergence of the culture. The ethnographer does this by immersing himself or herself in the location in order to examine the culture from the inside.

Through this participant-observation process, ethnographers collect field notes with descriptive reality from their perspective inside the culture. The descriptive field notes they take contain direct quotations from formal and informal conversations, and they contain the feelings, reactions, and reflections of the observer. These notes allow researchers to keep a record of their experience and to reexamine the experience. The ethnographer puts all the results of the accumulated knowledge together to share it with the community.

The reenactment experience gives instructors an opportunity to let their students experience a time-immersion situation. Through this experience students learn about social history beyond the headlines of history; the common people become real for students. They become immersed in the time period and feel what it would be like to live at that time.

Student interaction in events is particularly important in developing thinking skills. Reenactments set up a situation in which students react, participate, and interact while recreating a specific time period. When students discuss the drama event during and after the situation, the teacher leads the class to insights about what they experienced. Students also have an opportunity to pretend. At a time in life when peers and grown-ups are sending messages that it is not dignified to do so, students are encouraged, enticed, and incited to lose themselves in the world of historical re-creation.

For powerful learning students need to combine drama with history to learn history as they participate in drama. The experience of the participants is the concern of drama, and drama allows students to use many different situations to achieve experience with human relations. By introducing students to historical characters the student can form an intellectual bond between times. The ideas and perspectives of the characters become real when characters meet. Those performing with first-person historical narrative bring particular perspectives and generate both student questioning and empathic responses.

By working with characters and interacting formally and informally students acquire a multiple-perspective approach to issues and personalities. The students empathize with the perspectives, views, interpretations, and motivations of others. The reenactment experience acts to focus the issues of the time to the voices of the people.

Each person has the opportunity to share his or her opinion, whether as an individual or as a member of a representative group. These varieties of opinions provide practice for exploring issues, questions, and forming opinions in a manner similar to listening to others and examining their views, evaluating their statements, and choosing the best arguments. The political questions of the decade, the hopes, fears, ambitions, and foibles of the people are accessible to students in this manner.

STUDENTS ETHNOGRAPHERS LIVE IN A CULTURE TO DO RESEARCH THROUGH LIVED EXPERIENCE

The problems are real to the students, the energy and enthusiasm are contagious, and the learning environment is like-life. Students examine individuals within society, and students whose curiosity has been aroused examine events and emotions in a culture. People are the stuff of which history is made. The interaction between people and their world is a major advantage that allows the students to identify emotionally with the past. The universal link between people today and those of the past depends heavily on the ability of the students to empathize with the characters. Students discover real emotions and relations through the historical characters they portray, and the experience links the vital concerns of students across time from then to now.

The ultimate goal of living history requires immersion, stimulating all the senses, fully participating in a period of history, and feeling as if the participant is in a different time and place. Students work in a low-risk environment, practicing skills that apply in the world and are required to be empathetic in life; the students need to practice feeling. Students practice feeling empathy in history as a preparation for the future, and through reenacting situations students gather information about how people reacted, thought, and felt in a different time period.

REENACTMENT AS ETHNOGRAPHY

The culture of the historic period experienced in the reenactment is so varied and complicated that the experience is likely to be unique for each participant. This makes traditional objective and assessments extremely difficult to mesh with the experience of the reenactment. Ethnography asks what the nature of culture is. Students direct their own learning by asking four questions: What is the nature of the culture? What is the function of the culture? How is the culture transmitted? How does the culture emerge? By immersing themselves in the culture of the reenactments the student experiences culture from the inside. The student becomes a participant observer.

Students take mental field notes as they sort through their feelings, reflections, reactions, conversation, and descriptions of the event. When students leave the field they begin the process of writing and rewriting to tell the story of their lived experience. They call on their memory to interpret the culture and their reactions to it, and they record their most salient observations in description and detail. The narrative, guided by their four earlier questions, is the tool that assesses student understanding of what they experience. Students learn about culture through powerful teaching and learning of social studies using reenactment and ethnography.

FOUNDATIONS

When teaching social studies teachers help students learn about historical empathy. In this case historical empathy is the ability to understand the point of view of another person at another time and place. Teachers, regardless of the grade level, use literacy skills in social studies to help their students learn about historical empathy.[23] Even young students understand the passage of time and multiple sources through a variety of storybook accounts.

Students gather this knowledge through working with print and electronic media to synthesize information. Historical thinking comes from examining the source of the information from an author who has a point of view, further the information needs corroboration from additional source material. The students need to understand the context of the time when working with documents and multiple texts.

Role-taking experiences propel students to engage in dialogue before making meaning of history and citizenship. To do this, students engage in speaking and listening to identify with the enacted people and events. Students use role-taking experiences to learn about drama and historical reenactment.[24] Historical reenactment is laden with conflict that illustrates what has been lost to the participants in the modern world. Furthermore, experiencing the reenactment exposes the participant to the vulnerability of trying to navigate and construct meaning of the past. The emotional connection that reenactments provide the participants leads in the construction of empathy.

Some students use role-taking experiences to divest themselves of egocentrism and ethnocentrism. Students utilize world history content to reflect on individuals and groups by exploring global cultures. Cullinan et al. (2008) found that they could help students become more accepting of the differences found in other people.[25] Students explored diverse points of view from many people and locations around the globe to develop perspective consciousness. Students listened to other people and accorded their voices time and respect. Through listening to others students developed historic empathy skills and used skills of deliberation to examine their understanding of the world.

Students construct historical understanding when they examine multiple perspectives as a part of historical empathy. In role-taking students examine multiple perspectives and they encounter historical empathy. Fifth-grade teachers use inquiry, primary sources, and decision making in their classrooms to encourage the development of historical empathy.[26] The skills of decision making, inquiry, and the use of primary sources are key tools when engaging in deductive and inductive reasoning. Citizens in a democracy need these skills as they work for the common good. These are also the skills students use when they prepare for a simulation such as a historical reenactment.

CONCLUSIONS

Students need to find out about their community through experiences that allow them to relive events. Students develop their class community by engaging in common events and sharing experiences that allow them to explore the past. Students use dramatic experiences and events from their community's past. These students learn history that applies to their lives, and they learn about the people who live in their town; sometimes this even includes their relatives. Student solution seeking is the first step in community problem solving and civic efficacy, and students learn about history by experiencing a small segment of it in great detail through drama.

Students develop historical empathy when they work in community through literacy or speaking and listening experiences. Students abate egocentrism and ethnocentrism while examining multiple perspectives when they engage in role-taking. Teachers want to expose students to history at an early age so that students have an adequate context for understanding content.

Teachers use drama to encourage historical thinking and deep learning about the topics being studied in social studies class. Teachers want students to connect with their community, to understand what happened in it, and how it operated more than two centuries ago. Teachers give the students opportunities to explore history when students get to compare their present lifestyle to that of the past, and students focus on those things long ago and far away as being ripe for inquiry and wonder.

Teachers need to develop deep understandings and undertake rich experiences when they engage in historical reenactment as lived experience. Historical reenactment provides students with an opportunity for gathering the data of lived experience as ethnographers. While it is important to give students opportunities to explore history in depth, future study should concentrate on both the quality and quantity of information the students gather from this experience. Five powerful keys for teaching social studies are learned through reenactments while using ethnographic methods in the classroom. The reenactment helps students to use drama in learning both empathy and critical thinking; student ethnographers do both research and live in the culture.

NOTES

1. Julie, journal, May 7, 2005.
2. Mrs. M., individual interview, March 8, 2005.
3. National Council for the Social Studies, *Curriculum Standards for Social Studies: Expectations of Excellence* (Washington, DC: National Council for the Social Studies, 1994).
4. Jean Fritz, *"What's the Big Idea, Ben Franklin?"* (Logan, IA: Perfection Learning, 2001).
5. National Council for the Social Studies, *Curriculum Standards for Social Studies*.
6. Natalie, journal, May 12, 2005.
7. Ron, individual interview, May 24, 2005.
8. Pearl, journal, May 18, 2005.
9. Natalie, individual interview, May 22, 2005.
10. Julie, individual interview, May 23, 2005.
11. Natalie, journal, May 12, 2005.
12. Chris, journal, May 13, 2005.
13. John, individual interview, May 21, 2005.
14. Ron, journal, May 19, 2005.
15. Janet, individual interview, May 25, 2005.
16. Catherine, field notes, May 8, 2005.
17. Julie, field notes, May 8, 2005.
18. Transcript, May 8, 2005.
19. John, journal, May 18, 2005.
20. Natalie, journal, May 17, 2005.
21. Wayne, journal, May 16, 2005.
22. Dhaval, journal, May 15, 2005.
23. Thomas D. Fallace, Ashley D. Biscoe, and Jennifer L. Perry, "Second Graders Thinking Historically: Theory into Practice," *Journal of Social Studies Research* 31, 1 (2007): 44–53; Jeffery D. Nokes, "Aligning Literacy Practices in Secondary History Classes with Research on Learning," *Middle Grades Research Journal* 3, 3 (2008): 29–55.

24. Lisa Farley, "Repositioning Identification: Reflections on a Visit to Historica's Heritage Fair," *Canadian Journal of Education* 29, 4 (2006): 1019–38; F. Prediville and N. Toye, *Speaking and Listening through Drama 7–11* (Thousand Oaks, CA: Paul Chapman Publishing, 2007).

25. Beth Cullinan, Tim Dove, Robert Estice, and Janet Lanka, "Becoming Conscious of Different Perspectives," *Social Studies and the Young Learner* 20, 4 (2008): 18–21.

26. Teresa M. McCormick, "Fear, Panic, and Injustice: Executive Order 9066—A Lesson for Grades 4–6," *Social Education* 72, 5 (2008): 268–71; Teresa M. McCormick, "Letters from Trenton, 1776: Teaching with Primary Sources," *Social Studies and the Young Learner* 17, 2 (2004): 5–12; Gary Fentig, "Hard Times and New Deals: Teaching Fifth Graders about the Great Depression," *Social Education* 65, 1 (2001): 34–40.

4

✛

Pioneer Diversity
and Dissenters' Day

In the month of December the fourth-grade visitors to Conner Prairie experienced a treat when they engaged in a reenactment of Christmas Eve, December 24, 1836. The Midwestern pioneer village sponsored the Conner Prairie by Candlelight program to illustrate immigrants to the area and show the multiple traditions of these people based on cultural, ethnic, regional, religious, or national origins. In each log cabin or frame house students met a different person engaged in preparations for winter, celebrations, traditions, parties, Christmas, or deliberate noncelebration.

INTRODUCTION

Rather than teaching about pioneers as an isolated subject, teachers need to explain the conflict for the land as a contest for empire. The premise of the conflict was the clash of cultures with one hunting, gathering, and agrarian culture being displaced by another hunting, gathering, and agrarian culture. While some of the activities seem very basic, students who have been deprived of social studies in the primary grades need to talk about these ideas based on direct experience. While students are busy working with activities connected to a cultural universal, the volunteer leads them to talk about the context of the time.

The context of the time helps to set the discussion of the cultures in the fabric of world migration, national expansion, economic development, and political choices. Students find many of these issues controversial so they ask questions that lead them into future searches to find out more about the time and the people.

PIONEER DISSENTERS

The Indiana pioneer period was between 1780 and 1850. Since the Treaty of St. Mary's or the New Purchase that included Indianapolis was in 1824, it is best to select 1825 or after for the year of the reenactment. Once a time is established it is important to remain authentic to that time period. When teachers talk about pioneers and refer to inventions from after the Civil War or life in the early twentieth century, they lose the confidence of high-ability students and volunteers working with the reenactment. The teacher remains more credible and avoids misconceptions if they know what was appropriate for the pioneer period.

Authenticity also helps the students and teachers to concentrate on the story if there is a commonly agreed upon story shared between all participants (see table 4.1). When teachers use this story, they help set the time and place and clue the students into what they are supposed to do in the reenactment. More elaborate stories include dramatic elements or problems for the students to solve.

Some of these dramatic elements unfold in each segment of the day to help students find out what will happen next or gather information about a concluding experience. The work in each session connects to the story, or first-person characters come into the sessions to give dramatic vignettes to move the story forward. Some very elaborate stories have multiple characters visiting a session to interact with the students so that the story unfolds in front of their eyes.

The storyline helps move people around, explains social history, links the whole program, and gives purpose to the activity of the day. When scenes occur in different places, the students follow the character from one setting to the next; it is helpful to set up the scene so the students are

Table 4.1: Storyline

The year is 1825. Indianapolis, the recently named state capital, is just one year old, and Washington Street has stumps in the middle of it. Indiana has been a state for nine years, and Native Americans still live in the northern half of the state. Your family has purchased land in Perry Township because the land was cheap, and you could get clear title to the land. You live on a farm in Marion County, and your farm grows corn. You have horses, cows, chickens, sheep, and pigs that run wild. Your nearest neighbor is two miles away. School has ended now because there are crops to take care of; you get up at sunlight and work until dark. After sunset you put a candle in the lantern and prepare to sleep on the floor. You have one outfit of clothing and one pair of moccasins to wear. To survive you will work hard, and everything you own you will make with your own hands. You know much about life in 1825. The settlers in your community decided to build a new subscription school, and today you prepare to meet the schoolmaster. You do your regular chores of planting corn plus you need to cook a meal and make preparations to greet visitors who may be traveling through the area.

in the next area where an activity occurs. For example, in the Civil War reenactment a bugler signaled the change of program by sounding an advance. The students naturally gathered around the bugler to see what was happening; the bugler just happened to be where the next presentation or activity was about to begin.

The program flows smoothly in sequence as each first-person character develops and the storyline interweaves into each activity. The importance of each job explains and relates the events of the day to that storyline. The storyline makes the students anticipate the next scene through both prediction and informal discussion. Not thinking a scene through to its conclusion causes a lack of an ending.

Once the students enter the area many events take place. Students work on story problems using 1825 technology with pen and ink and slates, practice skills that meet state standards in story problems, and look at primary sources that inform them about the social rules of the time. Next they move into a round-robin collection of stations that help them look at broad concepts integral to each pioneer day, including clearing the land for food production with corn being the major crop, creating clothing from the raw product to the final good, looking at a skilled worker through blacksmithing, trade and transportation, or a simulation in which the students must select what they are going to take west.

Each station has a mini-activity plan including a primary source connection, materials, and procedures. Students discuss agricultural practices and take the crop from a stalk and process it into corn meal. They take this ingredient and combine it with others to create pioneer food that they may sample (see table 4.2). Students demonstrate how to clear the land and what they do with all of the extra wood (see table 4.3). After shearing the sheep the students use a multiple-step process until they have a finished product from the wool (see table 4.4). Students talk about transportation and trade. Some things they make for themselves and other things they must exchange with others. They may have items such as skins, which they trade for things they need (see table 4.5).

Not everyone will get to do all of these experiences, but by having multiple sessions the groups are small enough so that everyone gets to participate in something. The school cafeteria chefs create a special themed lunch that includes pioneer food. The special-class teachers create unique lessons that include information from major immigrant groups migrating to this area of the country including: folk songs from England, Ireland, Scotland, and Germany for music; German paper cutting for art class; and folk contra, line, and square dances for gym. The day concludes with a first-person presentation about a pioneer hunter on the frontier (see table 4.6).

Table 4.2: Corn Cultivation

Primary Source	Materials	Procedures
Diary of Calvin Fletcher[1] -Eating corn	Cold water Cream Salt Churn 2 bowls Butter paddle Paper plates Napkins Plow Hoe Grind stones Corn kernels Corn stalk Corn in husk Corn on the cob Corn meal Ingredients Match Firewood Charcoal Charcoal fluid Fire grill Iron skillet Hot pads Dish towels Trash bag Flipper Bowl Wooden spoons Measures	1. Churn butter 2. Use the buttermilk for the cornbread and the butter on the corn bread 3. Wash the butter and then add salt 4. Corn kernels 5. Plow: grub roots, around stumps and dead trees 6. Plant 7. Weed 8. Harvest 9. Husk corn 10. Hull corn 11. Grist mill: diagram 12. Grind corn 13. Cook: Corn bread, corn pone, ash cake, hoe cake, Johnnycake, corn oysters 14. Eat: (Some of the students will not like it)

Table 4.3: Clearing the Land

Primary Source	Materials	Procedures
The Journal of Lewis David von Schweinitz to Goshen, Bartholomew County, in 1831[2] -Clearing the land -Air pollution	Felling ax Log section Broad ax Adz Saw Sledgehammer Wedges	1. Girdling trees: Demonstrate 2. Shaping timbers: Demonstrate 3. Log rolling: Students clear land 4. Sawing: Wood for cabin furniture 5. Burning: Clearing the land 6. Split wood for fences (firewood)

Table 4.4:   **Sheep to Shawl**

Primary Source	Materials	Procedures
Documents of the Harmony Society[3]	Wool shears	1. Sheer wool
	Washtub	2. Pick wool
	Fels Naptha soap or Castle soap	3. Card wool
-Wool production	Raw wool	4. Spin wool
	Drying cloth	5. Dye wool
	Wool cards	6. Weave wool
	Drop spindles	7. Students model wool clothes
	Spinning wheel	
	Examples of wool dyes	
	Inkle loom	
	Wool pants	
	Wool shawl	

Table 4.5:   **Trade and Transportation**

Materials	Primary Source: *Travel Accounts of Indiana*[4]	10 cards per person
Roles	*Pioneer*	Eggs Skins Butter Hogs Whiskey
	Trader	Cloth Black powder Salt Coffee Lead
Procedures	1. Each person has a product or good 2. Each person has a price 3. Each person needs to make an advantageous trade 4. Each person needs 10 cards 5. Each person keeps record of each of their trades 6. Each person needs a modern price form	

STANDARDS

Across time people form groups; sometimes they are members of multiple groups at the same time. Even though they are members of groups they still maintain individual qualities and characteristics. Through participating in the reenactments students learn about National Council for the Social Studies Standards, including:

Table 4.6:   Pioneer Day Schedule

Time	Event	Activity
8:00 – 8:30	Education	Pen and ink: Copy *Washington's Rules of Civility*[5] Slates: Work story problems
8:30 – 12:30	Round robin stations	A. Corn cultivation B. Clearing the land C. Sheep to shawl D. Blacksmithing E. Pack a wagon F. Trade and transportation
12:30 – 1:00	Lunch	
1:00 – 1:30	Recess	
1:30 – 2:30	Special class	A. Music: Early American folk songs (English, Irish, Scottish, German) B. Art: German paper cutting C. Square dancing: Virginia Reel
2:30 - 3:30	Pioneer hunter	First-person presentation
3:30	Debriefing	
4:00	Depart	

- Time, Continuity, and Change
- People, Places, and Environments
- Individuals, Groups, and Institutions[6]

Students certainly learn about history of specific places, but they also learn about groups of people who came from different places and moved to new places. The students learn how individuals made contributions to their period of time and how these decisions impacted the other members of the community. Some decisions involved goods and services through production, consumption, and distribution.

EXAMPLES

Three examples of reenactments allow teachers to introduce groups, contrast them with other groups, and find commonalities between the groups. In these three examples a group of students examine pioneers, Native Americans, and nontraditional pioneers. Two volunteers work at each site to lead the activities when students spend twenty-four hours living a complete day as a pioneer (see table 4.7). Students spend most of their time in food preparation just as most of the life of the pioneer family would have been devoted to food preparation. For example, when work-

Table 4.7:　Twenty-Four Hours in 1825

Time	Event	Activity
Thursday 7:30 p.m.	Arrive at school	Dress in pioneer clothing
8:00 p.m.	Pioneer hunter	
9:00 p.m.	Folklore	
10:00 p.m.	Lights out	
Friday 6:00 a.m.	Wake	A. Biscuits
	Pack	B. Butter/milk/honey
	Restroom	C. Bacon
	Start breakfast	D. Eggs
		E. Ham
7:00 a.m.	Eat breakfast	
8:00 a.m.	Clean up	
8:30 a.m.	Session I [30-minute sessions]	A. Wooden toys:
		1. Dancing man
		2. Hoop and stick
		3. Stilts
		4. Corn cob darts
		B. Wood splitting
		C. Wooden toys:
		1. Jacob's ladder
		2. Cup and ball
		3. Tops
		4. Bowling
		5. Graces
		6. Buzz saw
		D. Pioneer clothing
10:30 a.m.	Restroom break	
10:40 a.m.	Session II [30-minute sessions]	A. Corn pone and potato soup
		B. Fried potatoes
		C. Gingerbread and leather breeches
		D. Hushpuppies
		E. Corn bread
1:00 p.m.	Restroom break	
	Lunch	
1:30 p.m.	Pioneer hunter: Two Snakes	
2:00 a.m.	Session III [30-minute sessions]	A. Wool rug
		B. Ice cream
		C. Plant garden (broom corn, gourds, flax)
		D. Hunter camp (deer hide, flint, and steel)
		E. Sampler
4:00 p.m.	Restroom break	
4:10 p.m.	Session IV [30-minute sessions]	A. Rope making
		B. Braided rug
		C. Soap making
		D. Sew straw tick mattress
6:00 p.m.	Clean up	
6:30 p.m.	Conclusions	
7:30 p.m.	Depart	

ing with a pioneer reenactment, after the cornbread goes into the Dutch oven to bake, the pans are washed, and the water is carried from the spring, the students have free time to play the game of graces.

The students need to participate in sustained contact with the symbols of the society through activities, jobs, and diversions. Students get to play with some pioneer toys, but they also spend time creating clothing, and working on tasks connected with providing shelter such as creating a straw-tick mattress or creating a wool rug. They get to work on farming, which helps them understand where their food comes from and how they are dependent upon creating a food supply that they can store for the winter.

To compare their experience as a pioneer with others who lived at the same time but in a different area of the state, the students participate in a Native American reenactment. The students involve themselves in a day filled with Native American lore, food, and activities, and the students live a day that resembles a typical day in the life of the historic woodland Native Americans (see table 4.8). Students include both agricultural and hunting traditions as they discover Native American food customs. The students spend a lot of time working with their food supply to determine where their food supply comes from and how to preserve it through the winter.

The students also engage in providing shelter through weaving mats and constructing a wigwam. The students do get to play some games, but the games are all dependent upon developing skills needed to perfect hunting. Students get an opportunity to construct Native American clothing and learn some cultural material such as dance steps to a nonsacred dance.

The Pioneer Dissenters' Day is an opportunity for students to learn that all of the pioneers did not think, look, or act alike (see table 4.9). Teachers tend to talk about the pioneers as if they were a monolithic group of people who had no differences. In fact, people on the frontier were as widely varied in their thoughts and actions then as people are now. They may have dressed differently or lived differently in intentional communities, and some of them lived better than the pioneers that students tend to recall. Through a first-person presentation students encounter an Owen community teacher. In their special classes they engage in diversity content in their art, computer, music, and physical education. In literature they read a story about Quakers.

In their computer class they determine when various immigrant groups of people came into the area, where they entered, and where they established black, Catholic, English, French, German, Irish, Jewish, Scotch, Swiss, or Welsh communities. In music class they learn about Moravian music. When the students meet the Shakers, they use metal pens and ink to re-create some of their mottos and sayings, and they use stencils to replicate designs from the period of time. The students solve labyrinths

Table 4.8:   Historic Woodland Indian Day

Time	Event	Activity
8:00 a.m.	Session I [20 minutes each]	A. Popcorn and buffalo stew B. Grind corn C. Basic Indian dance steps D. Drill rock and hand drill E. Games: 1. Spear and hoop 2. Bow and arrow 3. Spear
9:40 a.m.	Restroom break	
9:50 a.m.	Session II [20 minutes each]	A. Ribbon work B. Leather work C. Bead work D. Corn oysters E. Animal effigies
11:30 p.m.	Restroom break	
11:40 p.m.	Lunch	
12:15 p.m.	Session III [20 minutes each]	A. Build a wigwam B. Fry bread C. Harvest herbs D. Weave a cattail mat E. Double ball
1:55 p.m.	Restroom break	
2:05 p.m.	Session IV [20 minutes each]	A. Make clothing B. Carve a fish hook C. Make a rattle D. Rice cakes E. Scrape a skin and baskets
3:45 p.m.	Clean up	
4:00 p.m.	Debriefing	
4:15 p.m.	Depart for home	

when they learn about the Harmony Society. When the students meet the Amish, they create quilt squares and the whole group plays Amish corner ball in physical education.

ASSESSMENT

A great way to assess the impact of reenactment is to watch the students in action either on Grandparents' Day or when a guest school comes to visit. The students act as content experts to demonstrate and discuss what they have learned to an audience of peers or community members. With

Table 4.9:   Frontier Diversity Day

Event	Activity
First-person presentation: Joseph Neef Owen Community Teacher	
Session I	A. Make an Amish quilt square
	B. Shaker metal pen and ink to write a Shaker quotation
	C. Work a Harmony Society maze
Quaker Story: *Thy Friend Obadiah*[7]	
Special classes	A. Art: Use Shaker stencils
	B. Computer: Ethnic immigration research: Black, Catholic, English, French, German, Irish, Jewish, Scotch, Swiss, and Welsh
	C. Music: Moravian music
	D. Physical Education: Play Amish corner ball

practice and experience students are very capable of helping adults or other students have high-quality experiences. Students converse about food preparation and storage, clothing, and shelter, and they further discuss ideas and perspectives about their cultures. Students play as they act out these different roles and as they learn about people from different times and places.

For Grandparents' Day (see table 4.10) the students stay after school one evening to review where they will find their supplies and where they should set up their stations. They already know about the historic skill and what they have learned about it. On Grandparents' Day there is a free flow of people moving around from station to station while the two students at each post demonstrate tasks and talk about what they have learned. People move from station to station at their own pace, and students invite the grandparents to participate with them. During this time the students perform skills, present content, effectively communicate with grandparents and other visitors. By informing others they demonstrate their competence and understanding of the topics and their abilities to elucidate others.

For students from a visiting school (see table 4.11) the host students welcome the visiting students by talking about the difference between a log cabin and a log home. Then the host students describe the period clothing they are wearing; the visiting students break into small groups to work with a few of the students in each activity site. In the debriefing the host students ask the visiting students questions about what they have learned about the time period. By working side by side with their peers,

Table 4.10: Grandparents' Day

Time	Event	Activity
2:00 - 4:00 p.m.	Demonstration areas	Bead work
		Blab school
		Carding wool
		Herb garden tours
		Making apple pies
		Making biscuits
		Quilt block making
		Sewing a straw tick
		Splitting wood
		Spinning wheel
		Weaving

Table 4.11: Guest Student Program

Time	Event	Activity
2:20	Host students stay after school and change into pioneer clothing	Students set up for the program
3:15	The guest students arrive	Introduction to log home versus log cabin Introduction to the basics of 1820s fashion
3:30	Activities	A. split wood
		B. churn butter
		C. fried potatoes and gingerbread
		D. rope making
		E. wooden toys
3:45	Debriefing	
4:00	Guest students depart	Host students clean up and change
5:00	Depart	

the host students act as mentors and teach their peers about daily life in the pioneer era. Not only are the host students on display, but the visiting students are working with the host students to demonstrate their learned competency. The students perform assessment through peer teaching and working with peer mentors.

CAUTIONS

The greatest caution is that at the end of the day people are eager to get home, they are tired, and their rides are waiting. Do not, however, be in a hurry to see the students out the door. Reenactments without a debriefing session degenerate into just a series of hands-on activities with little intellectual content. It is the connections that the students make as they talk while they are doing the activity and the reflections of the students during the debriefing sessions that merit the effort of conducting a reenactment experience.

It may be beneficial depending on the length of the reenactment to have multiple debriefing sessions at different times of the day. It is also important to come back to the events of the day multiple times during the school year. Furthermore, the teacher previews the events of the day before the day begins, then talks with the students about what is happening during the day and why, and finally at the end of the day debriefs by discussing the impact and the implications the events of the day have had on everyone.

The debriefing, either oral or written, allows for students to reflect on the events of the day, connects what they have experienced to big ideas in the curriculum, and helps them remember significant events they then use in follow-up activities during the ensuing days or week. The teacher uses the debriefing time to help students determine significant individual actions and reactions from the group process. The debriefing sets the stage for turning experiences into knowledge, knowledge into product.

CIVICS CONNECTIONS

Civic literacy includes civic engagement, decision making, social issues, and the application of civic skills. Students are expected to show competency in economic literacy in order for them to make good personal decisions when working with money as well as understanding political decisions that impact upon public policy. What students do in educational experiences is often contradictory to what students are expected to do in the real world. Instead of analysis, participatory citizenship, and decision making students engage in passive tasks.[8] When students link social studies to the past, they find it to be relevant because of the opportunities for application.

In civic literacy students examine persistent social issues.[9] It takes imagination to examine persistent social issues and visualize what society might become. From civic literacy students should practice civic engagement where they are participating in society. The many suggestions for achieving this goal include: extracurricular, photographic projects for social action, conversations about institutional occlusions blocking educational reform, and elementary students use on line communication to directly comment to their state and national legislators of public issues.[10]

From extracurricular activities to direct involvement with government, students are expected to solve problems in a democracy. Students are also expected to show competency in civic literacy. It is important to have and practice specific civic literary subskills such as civic engagement in order to participate fully in society.

One way students learn civic engagement is through working with mentors. The mentors model the knowledge, skills, values, and dispositions that students need to experience in participating in society. Children value and identify with mentors as role models.[11] The engagement of students with members of their community is an important skill for students to learn as they work with new people and identify areas of common concern. Together they find ways to approach and solve problems in novel and unique ways. When students spend time together working on social studies–related activities, the students demonstrate civic competency.

Peer teaching seems to be good for children who come from a variety of backgrounds; it helps them to learn more and creates a better classroom climate. Students from various cultural backgrounds, ethnicities, and racial groups, including immigrants and nonnative speakers, find peer tutoring helpful. Peer tutoring assists students with a variety of learning backgrounds including ADHD, multicultural, multilingual, and urban locations.[12] Students engaged in peer coaching as well as peer tutoring demonstrate positive prosocial behaviors during unstructured time. Students find the interrelated learning environment brings both depth and discourse to their process.

Another way for students to learn about thinking is for them to engage in peer teaching and a thinking curriculum.[13] Each student makes a contribution through metacognitive processes, and student success in problem-based learning results in learning from everyone else. Elementary students and teachers feel the results of peer tutoring at other times in addition to during periods of social studies instruction. During unstructured time students who use peer tutoring in class experience more social approval and less social disapproval.[14] Students find that peer tutoring helps them improve their achievement in social studies. Teachers find that peer tutoring reduces off-task behavior in their students. Despite a variety of backgrounds, students who use peer tutoring in their classroom are thoughtful and happier.

When students do not receive adequate social studies experiences in the primary schools, the teacher of upper elementary or middle school is forced to reteach material the students should have had as a foundation for new information. When high-stakes tests push content out of the schools, teachers find themselves going back to teach cultural universals to physically more mature students. Teachers use cultural universals to introduce primary students to ideas about people who manifest a common idea in their respective lives regardless of time or place.[15] Teachers provide topical units about basic human needs to develop students' decision-making skills.

These powerful explorations of social experiences provide students relevant understandings of how they interact with their community. Teachers discuss many times the cultural universal of shelter with their students.[16] Teachers need to specifically teach the big ideas of cultural universals or student knowledge about these ideas remains undeveloped or nonexistent. Students do not learn cultural universals on the street. Teachers use cultural universals to teach about history and self-efficacy.[17] When teachers provide instruction in cultural universals that relate to historical content, they work with narratives, artifacts, timelines, and visuals. For students to develop historical appreciation and understanding the students need to engage in questioning. Since students can see how their life is involved in the community, they learn civic engagement and decision making.

CONCLUSIONS

Although it does not matter how a student participates in the reenactment, instruction occurs primarily in three possible time frames. In the first time frame, the reformed school day allows a reenactment for a period or a section of the school day. The school schedule modifies spatial needs, aides, tutors, lunch, and special classes to accommodate the activity. In the second time frame, the whole day includes a school day with either an extension in the morning or after school to allow people extra time for activities. Students experience the reenactment through resource people, special events, and time on-task.

In the final duration, a twenty-four-hour day gives the students time to feel the connections between sunlight and the work day. Students experience the centrality of a fire for heat and cooking as well as truly feeling the drudgery of carrying water and chopping wood to cook every meal. Students produce products, ideas, and beliefs, and they garnish a tremendous feeling of personal accomplishment when they finish their task satisfactorily. The students have a great deal of autonomy and responsibility for their learning in the reenactment.

Students engage in civic literacy when they work together to solve common problems. Students examine social concerns and controversial issues when they talk about many different people coming to the community. The students make decisions in work groups and examine past decisions made by others. The students find the content relevant because the pioneers come to look more like a modern community with a mix of people who did not always get along with one another. When students apply civic literacy, it means that they actively engage in civic skills when they analyze the participatory experiences they have through reenactment.

Students work side by side with adults to accomplish a common task when students work with mentors. Students enjoy working with adults, and the low ratio allows the adults time to listen to the students. Mentors help students learn knowledge, skills, values, and attributes when they participate in historical reenactments. The mentors help students find common concerns within society that they then work to redress. Students learn to solve problems in democracy when they work with a mentor, and mentors provide role models for demonstrating civic competency. Mentors play a key role in working with students during historic reenactments, and many guests perform in the first person by telling a historical narrative.

Students use peer teaching when they provide instruction to their age-mates who come to work with them in creative programs, when they learn food traditions, or discover construction details and clothing traditions. The students remain on-task and provide thoughtful interaction when they engage in peer teaching. Students enjoy the process and learn social studies content and skills. The students discourse in peer teaching, which allows them to learn more when they engage in historical reenactments. The learning environment provided by peer tutoring allows students to demonstrate depth of learning when they engage in historical reenactment.

Students use cultural universals when they participate in programs designed to learn about shelter, clothing, and food. Whether students experience cultural universals for the first time or it is a review of ideas first discussed in elementary school, students get real-life experiences when they work together in community. Culture universals are big ideas that students use to talk about multiple groups of people across time or space. Students work with cultural universals to spark questions, engage in decision making, and participate in civic engagement. Students have direct experience with these ideas as they experience and live with them during historical reenactments.

NOTES

1. Gail Thornbrough, Dorothy L. Riker, and Paula Corpuz, eds., *The Diary of Calvin Fletcher*, 1 (Indianapolis: Indiana Historical Society, 1972).

2. Lewis D. von Schintetz, *The Journey of Lewis David von Schweinitz to Goshen, Bartholomew County, in 1831* (Indianapolis: Indiana Historical Society, 1927).

3. Karl J. R. Arndt, ed., *A Documentary History of the Indiana Decade of the Harmony Society, 1814–1824*, 1 (Indianapolis: Indiana Historical Society, 1975).;

Karl J. R. Arndt, ed., *A Documentary History of the Indiana Decade of the Harmony Society, 1814–1824*, 2 (Indianapolis: Indiana Historical Society, 1975).

4. Shirley S. McCord, ed., *Travel Accounts of Indiana, 1679–1961: A Collection of Observations by Wayfaring Foreigners, Itinerants, and Peripatetic Hoosiers.* Indiana Historical Collections, 47 (Indianapolis: Indiana Historical Bureau, 1970).

5. *Washington's Rules of Civility*, www.history.org/Almanack/life/manners/rules2.cfm.

6. National Council for the Social Studies, *Curriculum Standards for Social Studies: Expectations of Excellence* (Washington, DC: National Council for the Social Studies, 1994).

7. Brinton Tukle, *Thy Friend, Obadiah* (London: Picture Puffins, 1982).

8. Beth C. Rubin and James M. Giarelli, eds., *Civic Education for Diverse Citizens in Global Times: Rethinking Theory and Practice* (Mahwah, NJ: Lawrence Erlbaum Associates, 2007).

9. Myra Zarnowshi, "The Thought Experiment: An Imaginative Way into Civic Literacy," *Social Studies* 100, 2 (2009): 55–62.

10. Linda Bennett and Julie Fessenden, "Citizenship through Online Communication," *Social Education* 70, 3 (2006): 144–46; Peter Thacker and Richard S. Christen, "Modeling Civic Engagement: A Student Conversation with Jonathan Kozol," *Educational Forum* 71, 1 (2006): 60–70; Nancy Wilson, Stefan Dasho, Anna C. Martin, Nina Wallerstein, Caroline C. Wang, and Meredith Minkler, "Engaging Young Adolescents in Social Action through Photovoice: The Youth Empowerment Strategies (YES!) Project," *Journal of Early Adolescence* 27, 2 (2007): 241–61.

11. Belle Liang, Renee Spencer, Deirdre Brogan, and Macarena Corral, "Mentoring Relationships from Early Adolescence through Emerging Adulthood: A Qualitative Analysis," *Journal of Vocational Behavior* 72, 2 (2008): 168–82.

12. Barbara N. Allison and Marsha L. Rehm, "Effective Teaching Strategies for Middle School Learners in Multicultural, Multilingual Classrooms," *Middle School Journal* 39, 2 (2007): 12–18; Ya-yo Lo and Gwendolyn Cartledge, "Total Class Peer Tutoring and Interdependent Group Oriented Contingency: Improving the Academic and Task Related Behaviors of Fourth-Grade Urban Students," *Education & Treatment of Children* 27, (3) (2004): 235–62; Pamela J. Plumer and Gary Stoner, "The Relative Effects of Classwide Peer Tutoring and Peer Coaching on the Positive Social Behaviors of Children with ADHD," *Journal of Attention Disorders* 9, 1 (2005): 290–300.

13. Ritu Dangwal and Preeti Kapur, "Children's Learning Processes Using Unsupervised 'Hole in the Wall' Computers in Shared Public Spaces," *Australasian Journal of Educational Technology* 24, 3 (2008): 339–54; Adina Shamir, Michal Zion, and Ornit Spector-Levi, "Peer Tutoring, Metacognitive Processes and Multimedia Problem-Based Learning: The Effect of Mediation Training on Critical Thinking," *Journal of Science Education and Technology* 17, 4 (2008): 384–98.

14. Tracy R. Lawson and Gabrielle Trapenberg, "The Effects of Implementing a Classwide Peer Tutoring Model on Social Approvals and Disapprovals Emitted during Unstructured Free Time," *Journal of Early and Intensive Behavior Intervention* 4, 2 (2007): 471–82.

15. Janet Alleman, Barbara Knighton, and Jere Brophy, "Social Studies: Incorporating All Children Using Community and Cultural Universals as the Center-

piece," *Journal of Learning Disabilities* 40, 2 (2007): 166–73; Jere Brophy and Janet Alleman, "Learning and Teaching about Cultural in Primary-Grade Social Studies," *Elementary School Journal* 103, 2 (2002): 99–114.

16. Jere Brophy and Janet Alleman, "Primary-Grade Students' Knowledge and Thinking about Native American and Pioneer Homes," *Theory and Research in Social Education* 28, 1 (2000): 96–120; Karon LeCompte, Sherry L. Field, and Janet Alleman, "Fruitful Collaboration: A Professional Development Project," *Social Studies and the Young Learner* 18, 2 (2005): 14–19; Robert L. Stevens and Melanie Starkey, "Teaching an Interdisciplinary Unit on Shelter," *Social Studies and the Young Learner* 20, 1 (2007): 6–10.

17. Janet Alleman and Jere Brophy, "History Is Alive: Teaching Young Children about Changes over Time," *Social Studies* 94, 3 (2003):107–10; Janet Alleman and Jere Brophy, "On the Menu: The Growth of Self-Efficacy," *Social Studies and the Young Learner* 12, 3 (2000): 15–19.

5

Community Celebrations and History Participation

The elementary-school students with their parents and their grandparents walked into the Union camp after being challenged by the picket. They visited the surgeon and his men prior to the anticipated battle the next day and watched as they sharpened their tools and checked their medical supplies. It was the family program entitled "The Night before the Battle," and it was set during the Civil War; here the students got to meet multiple people who would be engaged in the expected battle the next day.

The five-station walk allowed students to meet men on both sides of the Civil War. They included civilians who were busy taking shelter, black people who had taken the opportunity to liberate themselves by following the Union army, and profiteers who were trying to figure out a way to make a quick profit. Students and their parents learned about the multiple perspectives of people who found themselves involved in the Civil War.

INTRODUCTION

School is a place where families learn together when they engage in community events. These events are particularly designed to invite the community into the school so that members of the school district see how students are learning and how tax money is being spent. Even if the members of the greater community do not attend, photographs of the event with a news release often appear in the local newspaper to inform the members of the district that the schools play a role in the intellectual life of the school corporation.

Through these types of experiences students and their families learn material that corresponds to a variety of the National Council for the Social Studies standards including, Culture, Time, Continuity and Change, and People, Places, and Environments.[1] Families have experiences that allow them to share stories about how they lived in the past and how they celebrate traditions in the present. Families find out how other people live from other places and times and compare those experiences with their own experiences.

COMMUNITY LEARNING

In one suburb the area where the school was located and all of the surrounding land had been soybean fields for ten years before the school was built. Everyone was from somewhere else and there were very few ties to the community; thus, if there were to be a sense of community the school would need to play a major role in creating it. The school was naturally open for athletic events, but it needed to play a more important role in defining the sense of place. It became a place for all sorts of community services, from child care to scout groups. Its most important role was in developing a sense of intellectual community through stimulating programs.

Many types of family programs attempted to bring students, parents, and grandparents together. Some programs invited guest speakers to interact with a mixed-generation group to raise issues and talk about social issues. A Native American who was reared on a Canadian reservation, worked on high steel in the East, and then found his way into Western movies spoke about the many aspects of his life and the different jobs he had held. He talked about the regional differences between Indians and about stereotypes. Students, parents, and grandparents asked questions and learned together from their experiences.

In another experience a hobby turned into a multiple-sibling learning adventure that the entire community could share. One group of Boy Scouts made native clothing and did traditional-style dances. One of these scouts had a younger brother in the elementary school so the scouts came to school, demonstrated their skills, and taught those in the audience the dances they knew. They invited families to come out and join them and they instructed them while multiple generations participated. Here was a group of middle- and high-school students who were helping younger students as well as the people of their parents' and grandparents' age to learn something new.

A group of primarily female cloggers came to dance to traditional Appalachian tunes; they also taught all those in the audience who chose to join them in some of their steps. The dancers shared information about the music and the style of dance coming from a particular part of the

Table 5.1: Grandparents' Day—Moravian History and Culture

Time	Event	Activity	Location
5:00 p.m.	Costume fitting Greeter arrive Photographer arrive AV set up		
5:30 p.m.	Play practice		
	Quilt		Atrium
	Free-flow activities	A. 5-pointed stars B. paper chains C. string popcorn D. gold nuts	
	Stories of the Christmas past/ digital oral history project		Room #25
6:00/7:00 p.m.	Moravian history	Slide program	Cafeteria
6:15/7:15 p.m.	First Year in Hope, Indiana	Skit	Kindergarten
	Mary and Samuel's Christmas	Skit	Large group instruction
6:30/7:30 p.m.	Christmas candles		Room #23
	Christmas decorations and		
	Moravian display		Room #20
	Christmas candles		Room #23
	Folk craft		Room #24
	Moravian sugar cookies		Room #19
6:45/7:45 p.m.	Love feast		Room #29
	Moravian ginger cookies		Room #27
	Moravian sugar cake		Room #22
	Christmas stories		Library
7:00/8:00 p.m.	Christmas carols	Wooden recorder	Cabin
	Christmas by Luke		

country. Each of these programs invited multiple generations to learn more after school about the people who lived in their community. Many of the families had relatives who had come from this region recently or several generations in the past. The people in the community came to the school to learn as well as those who were enrolled in the school.

THE EXAMPLE OF GRANDPARENTS' DAY

Grandparents' Day (see table 5.1) provided an opportunity to engage in community education and the school became a place where all people could learn rather than just those who were within a particular space of chronology. The idea was that children should see that everyone learns, regardless of age or position in the family, and that interacting with multiple generations is pleasing. Siblings, multiple generations, and community members united for a couple of hours after school to learn together.

The theme of Grandparents' Day changed every year to include Mary Bryan's first winter in Indiana (see table 5.2), a mid-winter for William Conner's family (see table 5.3), holidays for the Calvin Fletcher family (see table 5.4), or even Moravian history.[2] There was a small Moravian congregation within the school attendance area, but the focus was on their history and culture.

Students involved in the programs arrived early to change into simple costumes. The audiovisual set-up crew checked to make sure that equipment was in the correct spaces for the evening. A designated photographer arrived to start setting up, checking light levels, and finding places for action shots. The greeter was positioned inside the door to orient visitors to the activities of the evening and to direct people to the program with the printed list of activities. The printed program listed the times and locations of each event, and there were purposely so many events that no event would become full. Because no one could attend all of the events in one evening, people had to choose what they wanted to attend.

While the students engaged in the last play practices before the audience arrived, parents and siblings experienced free-flow activities in the school foyer. The idea was to have a place where people could immediately become involved in the activities. It allowed people to arrive as they wished rather than on the program schedule, or they could find something to do while other events took place. These activities needed to be simple so everyone could become involved immediately. For those who wanted to try their hand at a traditional folk craft, a quilting frame was set up and all who wished to join were invited to quilt as they shared stories together.

The opening activities needed to reflect early- to mid-twentieth-century holiday customs that the grandparents might have experienced as a child. The group facilitator at these activities, in addition to giving instructions, got the various generations talking about their holiday experiences and traditions. As the participants recounted their memories the group facilitator suggested they may wish to preserve these memories. A digital oral-history recording booth was available in one of the rooms all evening for those who wanted to share stories with their grandchildren or children about past holiday experiences. All who participated in telling stories left the evening with a copy of their oral-history stories.

A group of students did research on the history of the Moravians in their state. Students wrote, narrated, and illustrated a PowerPoint program about Moravian history that they offered guests twice that evening.

Table 5.2:   Excerpt, Mary Bryan's First Winter in Indiana

Granddaughter:	Tell us again about your first Christmas in Indiana?
Mary Bryan:	Your father, Luke Bryan, was farming here and invited us to live in Indiana with him. Thomas, your uncle, had bought land in Franklin Township so we had two of our children in this area. Luke and your family came down and helped us pack the horses for the trip.
Samuel:	About ten o'clock in the morning we began our journey in a northerly direction in very cold weather. On an exceedingly narrow, steep road, made almost impassable by deep ruts, we wound our way slowly up the hills which everywhere skirt the Ohio more or less closely. Halfway up, in order to get past, we had to lend a helping hand to a wagon drawn by six oxen which had got stuck. The crest of the hills consists of vertical rocky walls. When one reaches the top, the country expands in a broad plain, with only here and there deep valleys of creeks and rivers, and one soon begins to admire the immense height and thickness of the trees. To be sure the woods are quite vast everywhere, but great was our astonishment at the quantity of land already in a high state of cultivation.
Mary:	We had a pretty good road for the first eight or twelve miles, as far as to a private house, where quite a refreshing dinner was served to us. From there on it became exceedingly difficult. For long distances it passes through wet, swampy through not infertile, beech wood, over an almost continuous so-called corduroy bridge, which was moreover, in a very ruinous condition, so that one was almost jolted to pieces. We traveled much on foot. The almost endless corduroy road was constantly interrupted by immense holes into which our wagon many times jolted down a foot and a half from the hard road, so that the horse sank to their bellies in mud: often they were in such a condition that it was impossible to get through at all. We then turned unhesitatingly into the most dense wood with tangles underbrush and after a long, roundabout way, winding between big, dense trees and fallen tree trunks we came back to the road scarcely one hundred paces from where we had entered it.
Samuel:	The same thing happened when fallen trees, often four or five feet in diameter, lay clear across the road. Needless to say, under such circumstances we progressed very slowly. Great dead trees, girdled and burned but still standing, are so numerous that anywhere else they would form a well forested tract. From there on, the badness of the road came to a climax and we approached Brush Creek, however due to the collapse of the bridge when we came up a large body of men who were reconstructing the bridge, called to us from afar that, if we would wait a short quarter of an hour, we might be the first to cross the new bridge.

Two groups of students presented two different plays at two different showings. These plays, based on primary sources, explained the historical context of the characters and explained how little the Moravians did to celebrate holidays, if they celebrated at all. With their work on this project

Table 5.3: Midwinter for William Conner's Family

William Conner:	In 1775 at Schoenbrunn, the Moravian center established three years before in eastern Ohio, Richard Conner and his wife were converted by the Moravian leader. The Conners, who were Presbyterians of Ulster origin, decided to engage in the profitable fur trade in the Indian country.
John Conner:	In 1801 both William and I were old enough to try our own hands at fur trading and came southward into the new Indiana territory which had been created in 1800 with a population of about 5,000.
William:	I decided to settle near the village of the Delaware Chief William Anderson and promptly married the chief's daughter. I established a trading post down White River from Anderson town, four miles south of the present site of Noblesville, which I founded.
John:	After the War of 1812 British influence steadily waned among the Indians. John Conner moved 20 miles up the west fork of Whitewater River and founded Fayette County and Connersville.
William:	In the meantime I had helped establish a Moravian mission near Anderstown. The Delaware invited missionary instruction, and Bethelehen sent out Abraham Luckenbach and Peter Kluge, who built a humble village.
Sarah:	Father I remember the visit we made to Hope.
William:	Do you?
Alice:	I remember the ginger cookies! They were so thin that they looked like paper. They had a creche which was a set of figures showing the holy family.
Sarah:	Before the service the whole town came together for a Love Feast. In a short time the young men had collected and piled up logs in the shape of an altar, which soon flamed up cheerfully. This was used to cook the love feast with which the sisters occupied themselves. The white cloth with which the sisters had adorned the table, for which one of them had gladly lent her handsome shawl, was removed for a moment in order that we might eat our refreshing dinner, consisting of cold roast chicken.
Mary:	The one hundred cups ordered in Philadelphia some time ago by Brother Martin arrived safely, as did an appropriate bell. They create general joy. The latter was used for the first time.
Alice:	At the feast, at which we sang German and English verses and had pleasant and grateful talk with general participation among the brethren and sister, was a love feast in deed and in truth.
Candy:	Soon the preparation of the Lord's Supper was completed. The communicants sat in a square; most of the mothers among them necessarily had their youngest children on their arms. All twenty persons, including ourselves, partook of the Lord's Supper.
Barbara:	We went to their log church with them at midnight. The drafts from the cracks in the walls and the floor made the bees wax candles with red crepe paper fringe dance as we listened as they sang to instruments. It was a lovely way to spend Christmas!

Table 5.4:   Excerpt Holidays for Calvin Fletcher's Family, Indianapolis, Indiana, 1817–1838

Calvin Fletcher:	Do you remember the Christmas of 1820? I went to Mr. Hill's for Sally. I had some talk with her on the road. I said that I felt very much depressed at this time on several accounts—I am rather uneasy—cannot but believe that if I were married I should be contented. In the evening I attended the concert where I enjoyed myself extremely well.
Sarah Hill Fletcher:	I remember the year of 1837. No school Christmas. Mr. K. and Dory and Martha all arose around 4 o'clock and went to prayer meeting. Louisa prepared breakfast. Aunt Betsy sent me a turkey for dinner and we had a big crowd to eat. I myself, I felt very disconsolate since James Cooley was sick.
James Cooley Fletcher:	I learned a lesson in 1823. The day was extremely cold, and I visited Mr. Henderson's and Blake's in the morning. I drank rather too much whiskey and brandy and ate too much sweet cake and came home and went to bed.
Elijah Timothy Fletcher:	Christmas of 1825 fell on a Sunday with cool weather and no snow on the ground. I went to hear Mr. Scott preach on the Methodist circuit with father, mother and James.
Calvin Fletcher Junior:	The Christmas of 1829 was the most exciting though. Christmas morning was cloudy and warm. At 4 o'clock Thomas Moore a boy of about 16 years of age living with us during the winter and going to school rose and my 3 oldest brothers. Mr. Ingram was also staying with us but was soon to leave for Lafayette where he expects to settle permanently. We did not have that usual firing of guns and parade that is usual. Temperance and Sabbath School societies have at this time in our place produced almost a calm. The Senate was meeting as usual and father was having with Brown and Cohern to assist a yellow woman and her three children who are claimed by her master a Virginian by the name of William Sewell. Sewell was detained in Indianapolis for a few days. Someone told the women she was free in Indiana as a free state and she left. He retook them and brought father into court. At 12 o'clock he went to the courthouse where the woman and her three girls, the oldest about 10 years, were brought forward. The house was full. Most of the members of the legislature were present. Great excitement among the people of the court. Their sympathies were alive for the women and children. Where the members of the legislature and some few who in our own place yet countenance the horrid traffic were almost clamorous for her to return to her owner. Witnesses were called on both sides. After the evidence was through father spoke in behalf of the women and read law. After father Mr. Wick spoke in opposition with much severity and abuse. Mr. Brown then answered and Hannagan closed for the claimant. Much prejudice was raised against several witnesses who testified in favor of the woman in consequence of the some intemperance language used by them while giving testimony. Trial closed about 8 o'clock at night and judge took time to give judgment.

the group of students helped to provide context to the audience outside their classroom.

For those interested in diving into a particular part of Moravian tradition, history, or culture there were two opportunities to get in-depth experiences in two different rounds of activities. Students helped an adult who facilitated each of these sessions.

In the first round, people had their choice of making Christmas candles, learning about Moravian Christmas decorations, making Moravian sugar cookies, or engaging in a Moravian folk craft. The second round gave people the choice of making Moravian ginger cookies, Moravian sugar cake, talking about the tradition of the Love Feast, or hearing Christmas stories in the library. The idea was to make intergenerational learning possible, engage people in their learning, and introduce new historical content and provide context for the participants.

Twice that evening students led groups to the reconstructed 1864 log cabin behind the school to hear a reading of the Christmas story found in the gospel of Luke. The students who had learned to play the recorder in fourth grade played Moravian carols around the fire. Parents, students, and grandparents all left the program with new ideas to think about and new historical figures to consider. The students played a significant role in providing programming to the group of visitors. Furthermore, students compared their mid-winter traditions with those of others to determine differences and similarities.

CAUTIONS

I once sat through a program about reenactment given by a group of students who had just returned from a day of doing historical reenactments. The teacher selected three students who had never questioned the teacher and obviously never thought of any mischief. The three teacher-pleasing students were passive, shy, quiet, and thoughtless. Unfortunately, they had not thought about their audience.

The students did not talk above a whisper, which made it impossible for the members of the audience to hear them. The unprepared students did not know what to say, how to say it, nor why it was important to say anything; the program was a colossal flop. I left without knowing any more than when I entered the program, and the rest of the audience left frustrated that they had experienced a program where they could not hear what occurred.

It is very important to talk about religion as history or literature rather than encouraging religion on public-school grounds. The events selected for the evening illustrated how one group celebrated holidays in the past. The events encouraged students to take leadership roles in teaching and also offered them opportunities to learn with their parents and grandparents. It was equally important to get families to talk about their holiday traditions and memories of the celebrations that they share. It was necessary to select a variety of themes that demonstrated religious traditions, lack of religious traditions, or secular celebrations rather than commercial celebration.

ASSESSMENT

When students create media presentations, participate in plays, lead activities, make music, or read, they are on display for the community. They deserve to be prepared for working with the public. They need content, skills, practice fielding questions, and direct experience before talking with a microphone. The community members then get to witness what the students have learned, and they comment on the presentations. Working with a real audience of mixed ages is more authentic than always reporting to their peers.

COMMUNITY AND ELEMENTARY SCHOOLS

Adults and students address many topics together through intergenerational learning, and while learning together students and seniors discover respect for each other as well as acquiring social values from the experience. In Taiwan senior citizens enjoy volunteering at the elementary-school toy clinic shop where they work with students and contribute to the school.[3] Seniors experience life-long learning and students realize the interdependence of the generations. Children and grandparents transfer knowledge between generations by facilitating change and encouraging cultural continuity.

Intergenerational learning supports language acquisition, reinforces knowledge learned in school, and places learning in a cultural context.[4] Seniors and students learn through service learning, and students thrive in a child-centered learning environment. Students and seniors learn important lessons concerning inclusion. Students work with seniors in sharing cultural heritage while modeling collaboration and socialization in the shared dining hall.[5] Students and seniors find mutual benefits as they learn together in an environment that is more similar to a democratic society.

The intergenerational interaction helps multiple generations learn from cultural studies. The mixing of generations helps develop the human resources from both children and the elderly. The elderly provide a long-term perspective that provides stability and a broad perspective on the education of the student.

The faculty members of schools need to provide space for family learning. This opportunity needs to entice multiple members of the family to come to the school; they need to be particularly solicitous to those who are unwilling to come. Fathers are not typically attracted to school functions, as witnessed by matriarchical Parent Teacher Organizations or Associations. The decision is not usually an individual choice but rather cultural and social.[6] A variety of creative solutions needs to be found to provide services to both mothers and fathers.

To say that parental involvement is important is a cliché, but Hurt (2000) describes how students and parents benefit from parental involvement.[7] Parent outreach is predicated on a welcoming environment and attitude. Fathers and mothers both need opportunities to learn along with grandfathers, grandmothers, and students in the schools. A variety of programming that is of interest to the entire family helps bring in a variety of family members.

Community events are an important part in the life of students and families; these events provide intellectual enrichment and academic stimulation. Elementary-school faculty members capitalize on these enrichment opportunities. Effective principals promote academic community events while college students who are mentoring young students assist with community events.[8] College students and school staff help connect students with community events. The community events that students experience help to connect them into life within the neighborhood. Community celebrations are important so students see people finding connections that they share with others.

Community celebrations range from historical events to local attempts to boost and celebrate people, places, or ideas. Local events such as Levi Coffin Days, the Covered Bridge Festival, or the Steam Harvest Festival all grace the calendar. Students examine events such as the celebration of the Lewis and Clark expedition and then determine how interpretations change across time.[9] This type of community celebration shapes the students' understanding of the national context. Students see connections to the community through local or national festivals.

Community development is an important job, especially in rural areas, small towns, and inner-city schools. Students and school faculty provide key support in the form of ability and energy to develop the potential of the community. School members take a leadership role in community development; local teachers especially make connections to the community they serve.[10] Professional community and practitioner constituent interactions occur when teachers live and work in the same school corporation.

By having a stake in the community where their home is located, the teachers meet people in their daily contacts, and they harness these network contacts to accomplish tasks in the community. It does not take the action of the mayor to accomplish a task, but knowing a small group of committed volunteers can be more effective in influencing local politics.

CONCLUSIONS

Students, parents, and grandparents engage in intergenerational learning. Students who have common experiences, discussions, and activities build connections with people in addition to their peers. Whole families learn that school is a place where everyone regardless of age gains knowledge. Students model learning from their parents and grandparents, and furthermore they model learning for their younger siblings. Students thus see their younger and older siblings learning with them and their teacher learning with their students.

Schools are a place where families learn together; they learn from one another about different people, places, and times. They particularly find out about the past from one another through opportunities to talk about their family history and traditions. Students take this time to acknowledge the connection between their family history and the larger context of history. The family members compare their experiences to the circumstances that other people faced. The school allows the family to share their history as a recognized part of a national story.

Students engage in community events to discover a sense of place and find that their community had a role in the past. Many unique events occurred in the students' own community, whether it is defined as a state, county, or village. Students learn about these events and find how different people see these same events through multiple perspectives. Communities still have events, and students get to attend these events where they get to witness the interaction of individuals with their peers. Students witness and participate as community members when they replay former events and create new traditions.

Students engage in multiple examples of community celebrations that tie them to immediate people, events, and places. The celebrations in which the students participate connect them to the schools. The celebration of an individual, group, or hobby helps students have a variety of experiences that serve to enrich their lives. Involving people from both within and outside of school helps to define the community and the relationship the student has to it. A community celebration includes multiple activities that promote the multiple perspectives, groups, and cultures represented in the community.

The thoughts and dreams of education move into other aspects of building a community when schools become a place where community development occurs. The school as an intellectual institution provides leaders and talent for originating community-based solution seeking. Community members find opportunities to volunteer as well as a place for intellectual enrichment. Students meet with members of the community who plant the seeds for service-learning activities. Students recognize community issues and seek solutions to redress those problems through direct action.

NOTES

1. National Council for the Social Studies, *Curriculum Standards for Social Studies: Expectations of Excellence* (Washington, DC: National Council for the Social Studies, 1994).

2. Gail Thornbrough, Dorothy L. Riker, and Paula Corpuz, eds., *The Diary of Calvin Fletcher, 1* (Indianapolis: Indiana Historical Society, 1972).

3. Jon-Chao Hong, Ming-Yueh Hwang, Hwey-Wen Liang, and Hsin-Wu Chang, "A Toy Clinic Shop: Innovation Management in a Shin-Tai Elementary School," *Educational Gerontology* 34, 11 (2008): 1018–33.

4. Charmian Kenner, Mahera Ruby, John Jessel, Eve Gregory, and Tehera Ariu, "Intergenerational Learning between Children and Grandparents in East London," *Journal of Early Childhood Research* 5, 3 (2007): 219–43.

5. Chandra Fernando, "A Visit to a Montessori Elementary Class in Israel," *Montessori Life: A Publication of the American Montessori Society* 18, 4 (2006): 26–28.

6. Flora Macleod, "Why Fathers Are Not Attracted to Family Learning Groups?" *Early Child Development and Care* 178, 7–8 (2008): 773–83.

7. Judith A. Hurt, "Create a Parent Place: Make the Invitation for Family Involvement Real," *Young Children* 55, 5 (2000): 88–92.

8. Joan B. Anderson, "Principals' Role and Public Primary Schools' Effectiveness in Four Latin American Cities," *Elementary School Journal* 109, 1 (2008): 36–60; Mary Trepanier-Street, "Mentoring Young Children: Impact on College Students," *Childhood Education* 84, 1 (2007): 15–19.

9. M. Trofanenko, "More than a Single Best Narrative: Collective History and the Transformation of Historical Consciousness," *Curriculum Inquiry* 38, 5 (2008): 579–603.

10. Wayne A. Reed, "The Bridge Is Built: The Role of Local Teachers in an Urban Elementary School," *School Community Journal* 19, 1 (2009): 59–76.

6

✦

Learning from a Community Festival or Reenactment

"I think that the Indians didn't have much power because the white people, the settlers, were very much in control. Usually . . . [the settlers] were a lot stronger than . . . [Indians] because they were . . . more prepared. They were usually the ones who had guns. . . . The settlers had most of the power. Usually the people who were in control . . . have a little more power, like the people in political parties."[1]

Elementary-school students selected topics that interested them and planned their itinerary for attending a reenactment. They spent one day in the fall attending a community festival plus class time to prepare and debrief from that event. Students attended the Feast of the Hunters' Moon depicting the international fur trade in the 1700s, an annual rendezvous between Native Americans and French Traders.[2] Global trade networks brought people of differing ethnic backgrounds together in mutually advantageous economic contacts. Students gain knowledge about who was involved with the trade and how it worked when they visited the festival.

> The English and the French . . . liked beavers for top hats and so . . . they came over here so that they could trade what they had with the Indians to get what they had which was the beaver skins so they could take it back over to Europe so they could make hats and get a lot of money.[3]

Students discerned many things from the events at the festival, the storytelling, and the reenactment, including how events and daily life compared between multiple groups in the area at the time. Students got

69

an ethical sense of events as they evaluated for themselves what they thought was good for society.

> I think it was unfair for most of the people because a lot of people took their land because they thought they could not do anything about it . . . soldiers or people who needed new land took the Indians' land.[4]

Students met and made connections between Scots, Irish, and Native American populations who had all been despoiled of their lands. Students attended this event to learn more about colonial content, decision-making skills, evaluating programs, and establishing priorities. Students planned the educational events and activities of their day and then acted on their plan when they practiced consensus building, negotiation, finding common ground, and compromise in making decisions.

LEARNING AT A FESTIVAL

Students made decisions about what and how they learned in this introductory inquiry experience based on democratic citizenship. For a class field trip students determined where they went, what they learned, how they budgeted their time, and how they shared what they learned with others in their class. Students in this inquiry experience took control of their learning because they had power over it; it was their questions for which they sought answers. Many different events occurred on the site of the festival, and students made wise decisions with their time to learn from the event. By getting the opportunities to make decisions they practiced important citizenship skills.

The teacher previewed the daily schedule and provided an example arena schedule for the students by highlighting what was available to see and do while stressing events they valued (see tables 6.1, 6.2, 6.3, 6.4, 6.5, 6.6, and 6.7).[5] At this time the teacher provided a purpose for celebrating the annual trading meeting between cultures at the event, told why the teacher wanted to take the students to see this, and explained why the students needed to learn decision-making and negotiation skills.

The teacher wanted the students to have enough information to make informed decisions and shared her priorities, but she did not expect all the students to follow her lead. As the students heard about events that interested them, they felt led to go their own directions; the daily events schedule listed all events that involved the entire site. The teacher allowed students to set their own priorities for leaning within the context of the time period, because the teacher trusted her students to make meaning from the site. As coconstructors of the learning experience the students determined the parts of the program that interested them the most.

Table 6.1: Children's Activities Schedule

Site	Activity
122	Making music booth
138	Tippecanoe County Historical Association storytelling booth
143	Pottery
145	Candle making booth
150	Children's bead booth
210	Tomahawk throw
219	Children's costume try-on
220	Children's trade blanket
221	Wigwam village
223	Children's gifts
224	Toy demonstration
339	Native American stories
350	Woodturning
351	Cross-cut sawing
360	Rope making
376	Osage Orange catapult
457	Rope making

Table 6.2: Programs on Grounds Schedule

Time	Event	Location
All Day	Exhibit and Traders House	Blockhouse
9:15	Cannon demonstration	Artillery park
10:00	Opening ceremonies	Flagpoles
11:00	Landing of the Voyageurs	Boat ramp
11:00	French stories	Wigwam Village
12:00	Flintlock reliability contest	Artillery park
1:00	Tomahawk throw	Tomahawk range
2:00	Canoe races	Boat ramp
3:00	Cannon demonstration	Artillery park
3:00	Native American stories	Wigwam village
5:00	Closing ceremonies	Flagpoles

Students formed groups of three, and in these groups they prepared, experienced the site, and debriefed together. Using the schedules students needed to individually prioritize all the events to determine what interested them the most (see tables 6.1, 6.2, 6.3, 6.4, 6.5, 6.6, and 6.7). The teacher provided the schedules of events for the day, including multiple

Table 6.3: Voyageur Stage Schedule

Time	Event
10:30	Colonel Webb's Band of Musick
11:30	Trois Canards
12:30	Barb Kotula Szeszycki
1:30	Northland Voyageur Choir
2:30	Hogeye Navvy
3:30	Wild Geese

Table 6.4: Landing Area Schedule

Time	Event
9:00	Dr. Theodpulus Von Gerlach
9:45	Sperreng Fiddlers
10:45	Native American hand games
11:15	Voyageur Ancient Fife and Drum
12:00	First Michigan Fife and Drum Corps
12:45	Janesville Fife and Drum Corps
1:30	Great River Fife and Drum Corps
2:15	River Valley Colonials
3:00	Tecumseh Fiddlers
3:45	Strolling Singers

Table 6.5: Military Drill Field Schedule

Time	Event
9:00	Theatiki Fife and Drum Corps
9:45	LaCrosse demonstration
10:45	42nd Royal Highlanders
11:15	Old Guard Fife and Drum Corps
12:00	Tippecanoe Ancient Fife and Drum Corps
12:45	French Fashion Show—Forces
1:30	Tactical Demonstration—Forces
2:15	Northwest Territorial Alliance Fashion Show
3:00	Highland Games
3:45	Massed field music

concurrent events and some whole-site events. In addition, she included the one-time events, repeating events, and continuous events. The site also included traders, campsites, musical groups, educational activities,

Table 6.6:   River Arena Schedule

Time	Event
9:00	Oxen
10:45	Hoosier Ladies Aside
11:30	Bush Family Dancers
12:30	Madam Cadillac Dancers
1:30	Iroquois Singers and Dancers
2:30	Calumet Ceremony
3:15	Spirit Wind Singers and Dancers
4:00	Heritage Musik and Dance

Table 6.7:   Block House Schedule

Time	Event
10:30	Bittersweet and Briers
11:30	Father, Son, and Friends
12:30	Dean Shostak
1:30	Bent Nickel Dance Band
2:30	Traveler's Dream
3:30	Highland Reign
4:15	Newfoundland Program Dogs

and military groups. Representatives presented many educational events from a variety of nationalities including English, French, Native American, and Scots.

PREPARATION

After students individually prioritized the events they most wished to attend, they met with their two peers and as a group of three they took turns comparing their lists and planning their day (see table 6.8). They determined what interests they shared in common and on what events they immediately agreed. Students needed to use all of the arena schedules to plan how to spend their day, and they used their arena schedules to find events they wished to attend, such as Kevin Stonerock's first-person presentation of a pioneer trader.[6] First, they established what they all wished to attend by consensus.

Through negotiation and compromising the groups of three next found common ground to determine what they wanted to do as a group. They

Table 6.8: Student Schedule

Time	Location	Event
9:45	LaCrosse demonstration	Military drill field
11:00	Landing of the Voyageurs	Boat ramp
12:00	First Michigan Fife & Drum Corps	Landing area
1:30	Tactical demonstration	Military drill field
3:00	Cannon demonstration	Artillery park

traded sites: "I will go to yours if you will go to mine." They yielded to another student's desire, or they yielded to the interests of a majority of the two students. After negotiations they made three copies of their plan for the day. Next the teacher reviewed the map of the reenactment site including natural features, boundaries, meeting sites, and where students could find the events listed in their plans (see figure 6.1).[7] Students evaluated their plan to see if it were possible to do all of the things they had planned after seeing the maps.

They made changes before giving the teacher a copy of their final plan, but each student also kept a copy of the list and map for themselves. With this plan their group navigated through the site and attended the events that interested them the most. They started practicing negations and decision making in the classroom, established a plan for their learning, and evaluated their plan.

ON THE SITE OF THE FESTIVAL

On the site of the festival the teacher reminded the students of the procedures necessary for making the day run smoothly. Each student had a watch, knew how to tell time, and agreed when to meet at the end of the day. Each student assumed responsibility for being prompt and avoided having others wait for them. The teacher reminded the students of the fenced site boundaries where the students may go. The teacher also pointed out areas that the students needed to avoid such as the river and the steep banks; the students assumed responsibility for staying within the boundaries and avoiding hazards.

Once on site the teacher and the students established a common meeting place, and adult chaperones took turns staying at this station so there was continuous coverage at this point. Students knew they could meet an adult here at any time if they needed assistance; this provided a safety net for the students so they knew aid was always close at hand. All three students stayed together for the entire day; if they did become separated,

Figure 6.1: Map of Site

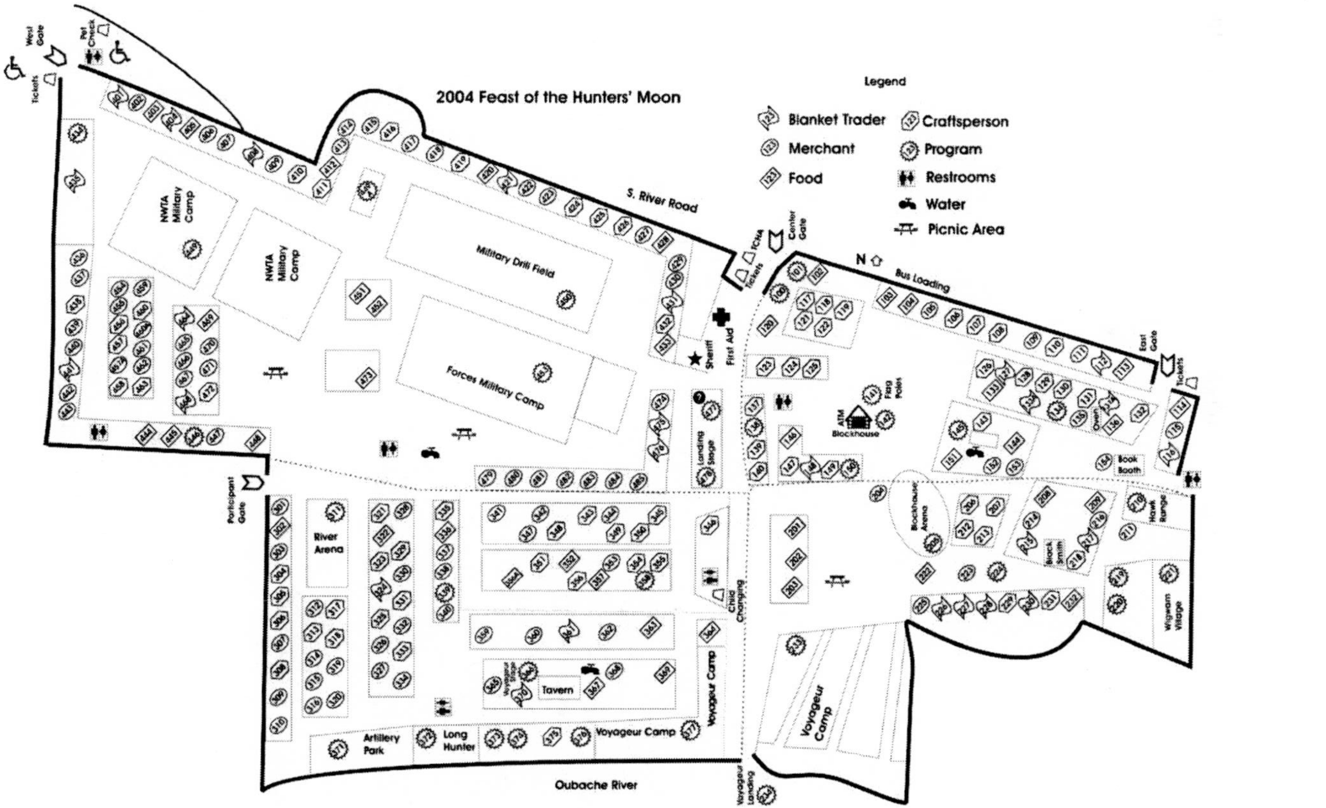

Legend

- Blanket Trader
- Merchant
- Food
- Craftsperson
- Program
- Restrooms
- Water
- Picnic Area

2004 Feast of the Hunters' Moon

they immediately went to the meeting area so that they could reunite. Students could not get lost or stay lost this way, and they therefore did not wander the grounds by themselves.

Teachers reminded the students of reenactment etiquette, which required a wide berth be given to a tent if it was closed, but if it was open it was alright to peer in and examine it. Students were also advised when talking to participants that they should refer to period garments as "clothing" rather than "costumes." At that point students followed their schedule for the day at the Feast of the Hunter's Moon.

POTENTIAL PROBLEMS

The most pleasant day at a community festival can look dark if an unforeseen event emerges; a change in the weather can make the day uncomfortably cold and windy, rainy, or hot. Dressing in layers and being prepared to be outside can prevent weather from becoming a disaster. Minor first aid may be needed for insect bites or stings, scraped knees, or sunburn; check the site map to locate the first aid stand. Students have been known to lose a quantity of money or personal belongings. Carry an extra sack lunch so no student is hungry during the day; direct the students to the lost-and-found station at the end of the day as the need arises.

When a student is missing at the end of the day the student is usually fine, but the teacher tends to panic. Remember as the crowd thins and departs it becomes progressively easier to search and find a student. While it seems calamitous, students usually turn up in less than thirty minutes. The most common problem is, because of height, students neither see nor hear, but students tend to move through crowds until they can see and hear. Students need to remember though that they need to share the festival with others by demonstrating consideration of others, moderating the volume of their voices, limiting horse play, and moving carefully through crowds.

DEBRIEFING

Students successfully navigated through the site charged with their own learning, and they seemed eager to share the results of their day. When the students returned to the class, they evaluated the experience through four questions in small groups and through individual journal writing. The four questions that guided their day were: "What was missing?" "What was inaccurate?" "What did they get right?" "How much was historically inspired entertainment?" Students were also eager to comment on what they enjoyed, what they saw, and what they did.

Students were asked to move beyond the superficial and the fun aspects of the day and comment with a critical eye about what they had learned. Teachers asked students to comment on the historically themed events to determine how much was entertainment in comparison to the amount of documentation of social history. This critical perspective allowed them to sort their impressions of the day into facts, concepts, and generalizations about life in that time and place.

Students were surprised not only with what they saw but also with what they did not see at the Feast. Their comments about the Feast noted what was missing from the event that they would have predicted they might have seen. "We did not see that many Indians."[8] Cole realized that at that time there would have been many more Native Americans at the event than Europeans. Students commented about the lack of controversial issues available for exploration in this event. They may notice the lack of animals and animal waste, necessities at that time but offensive to the twenty-first-century visitor and banned by modern health ordinances.

Back then they did not have cars and they have cars here. I think they would have horses. When Mrs. J. took us to go see the Indian tribe down there I bet we would have seen horses like the animals they had back then.[9]

Students commented on the lack of transportation to get all of these people to an event of that time. Even fairly young, unsophisticated students can determine a representation of uncritical history. "Well, they had boats there, but I thought they would ride horses."[10] Students could also mention the good health, good teeth, cleanliness, lack of odors, and lack of smallpox scars on the participants at this festival. Students might also comment on people who were missing and their stories, which they did not hear at the festival. Students questioned their experience by discussing what they thought they would have seen at this site.

As students evaluated inaccuracies they found at the site, they mentioned trash cans, fresh water sources, and waste removal. While none of these services were authentic, twenty-first-century participants and health regulations demand them. Students also mentioned period clothing.

They were not that strict on your costume so there's like a lot of people who were not in the correct time period clothes. A lot of the booths need workers so if your costume wasn't exactly accurate they weren't [quite] that picky . . . some of the events they do are not period like the tomahawk throwing." (Chelesse, fifth grade)

Once the students started questioning period clothing they also started questioning events they saw. The students noticed a difference in dress between the people they deemed to be experts and others on the festival grounds. "I think it might have been a little bit different because the people dressed differently; there are not many people wearing things like Mrs. J. [the teacher] or the volunteers."[11] The participants have a subculture uniform complete with their displayed multiple-year Feast-participant pins.

Students also called attention to housing that raised questions in their minds. "I really did not expect as many teepees as we saw."[12] A teepee would have been an abnormality in the eastern woodland tradition. Students questioned inaccuracies on the site due to twenty-first-century sensibilities and sloppy reenactment.

Students also evaluated what the event did right and why this is a high-quality event that has been successful for decades. First, the students looked at the structures and majority of the period clothing. "The way they dressed and the way they had their things built I think from what Mrs. R. taught us they got pretty accurate about the houses."[13] On the whole the festival set the scene correctly, and they agreed that the festival interpreted a river transportation and commerce gathering well.

Students carried away the idea of an international trade network based on beaver skins and river trade. "I did not really know if I would find any canoes and I found them here."[14] Water transportation was the easiest way to get around and the students got that idea from the site. Students then summarized and discussed their experiences, how their plans worked, how they made decisions, and how they evaluated the success of their plans.

They also evaluated the success of negotiations in satisfying all of their group members. "It is kind of celebrating the day in history. The students enjoyed the choices that they made and enjoyed all of the crafts they got to see demonstrated. They made good plans and even though the negotiation was sometimes difficult they agreed that they made good decisions. It is a day when we can all dress up and be . . . eighteenth-century people."[15]

FOUNDATIONS

Community festivals allow student opportunities to meet key contact people and investigate local resources. Furthermore, the excitement of the social festival is infectious; it encourages learning among people of multiple ages in a common area. Festivals serve to define the community, transmit culture, and allow the community to participate in education.[16] The meeting of specialized resource people such as reenactors, who are content experts in their field, is always an advantage of the event.

Students can work with these experts in the field to conduct a research situation. The field trip is a research activity in which students gather information to be shared in the classroom with their peers.[17] This research is directly connected to their community and their sense of place. Finally, the experience of being surrounded by a cadre of dedicated experts and seeing another type of community is exhilarating. Students learn with and from members of the community when they experience festivals.

Traditionally students exercise no choices but passively move through rotations between tour stops.[18] Students learn lists of facts, stringing together isolated and disjointed information to be memorized and later repeated verbatim. Most of the time students are the recipients of information rather than being actively involved in the constructors of knowledge. While students may make connections to their class work if their teacher is present, a teacher-directed interpretation of the site remains dependent upon the role of the teacher to modify the experienced through their version.

These students became involved with question generation that they could then discuss with their teacher, but students lacked adequate preparations and background knowledge for what they were seeing. Student experiences with visual, verbal, or tactile field-trip lessons are poorly prepared.[19] Few, if any, controversial issues were encountered and students moved through the feel-good history site with less-than-critical eyes. Prior preparation is needed to make students aware of the questions they need to ask and the issues they need to explore on site.

In addition to the detriment of taking time from class and paying for both transportation and the gate fee, the students spent time at the trader store purchasing souvenirs, and also stopped for concession drinks and snacks. The result of these compounding costs totaled a very expensive day for both students and teachers. In an ever-tightening economy members of a school community need to find field trips that meet educational needs and maximize time at a low cost to teacher and students.

More and more school districts are cutting field trips to balance their diminishing educational budgets.[20] Teachers need to realize that the role of the field trip is to expose students to what they have not experienced before and what they are not likely to learn with members of their family. The teacher acts to create a learning environment in and out of the classroom where students can learn and explore while expanding their horizons.

Many field trips are very teacher-planned, -directed, and -led, but teachers who let students plan and execute their own field trips are more likely to provide their students with inquiry experiences. Inquiry is a process in which students define a problem and then seek to find a solution to that problem.[21] This means there will be ambiguity and doubt, it will be open ended, and students will "own" the problem. As students seek answers they will investigate and reach a conclusion. The teacher's role is to help gather resources for students and to work with them, but neither the teacher nor the students know exactly the resolution of an inquiry when they start.

CONCLUSIONS

Of course, not everyone will concur with this method of teaching. Some educators will resist the ideas of students having input into their education while others will resist the teacher giving up direct instruction with the students. Heavy chaperone involvement for preschool-age groups make field trips more like family visits with parent–child interaction, and also rejects assignments that make the museum more like school.[22]

The maturation of students and the developmentally appropriate nature of those who are ready to cut more strings from parents and adults make this type of autonomous learning more appealing for older rather than younger students. Older students certainly are ready to strike out in small groups to investigate. While a festival is a good way to integrate inquiry methods into student field trips, it is not the only way to take a field trip and other types of sites would require different methods.

Social studies educators do need to promote inquiry to encourage students to hold problems as their own. Students need suggestions and limits set by teachers on where to go, what to do, and how to do it. The students connected their prior knowledge with new learning.[23] Students are able to take what they learned in preparation from the classroom and connect it to what they have learned at a festival. By giving students some latitude in selecting an assignment that motivates them, teachers encourage decision-making skills through this event. Students are required to make a number of choices prior to engaging in the field trip, and students must think on their feet as the day unfolds.

Students are required to do history not to just passively receive it when they are involved in inquiry-based projects.[24] They apply a critical lens to the festival to evaluate what they are seeing and experiencing. As students make choices about what they will learn at a festival, they are conducting research as they gather information and experiences to bring back to the classrooms from the event.

When students work in small groups the members of their peer group modify their research project as they plan and attend the festival. By working in a group and staying in a group on a festival site students practice finding common ground for solving problems through negotiation, compromising, and reaching consensus. Inquiry requires students to raise questions, use logical reasoning, and conduct research.[25] The environment of a festival requires students to raise questions about what they are seeing, use logical reasoning to determine conclusions, and conduct research on the site to gather information.

In their groups students must raise questions about the sites they are seeing at the festival, use logical reasoning to determine if their plan is working at the festival, and conduct research about how their group worked while they were at the festival. While at the festival the students used democratic problem solving skills to negotiate, organize, and carry out a plan that required compromise that allowed all members of the group to enjoy consensus.

NOTES

1. Chelesse, fifth grade, individual interview, October 14, 2004.
2. Feast of the Hunter's Moon, www.tcha.mus.in.us/feast.htm.
3. Calib, fourth grade, individual interview, October 13, 2004.
4. Kendra, fifth grade, individual interview, October 14, 2004.
5. Children's Activities, www.tcha.mus.in.us/children.htm; programs, www.tcha.mus.in.us/programs.htm.
6. Kevin Stonerock, www.kevinstonerock.com/Livinghistory.html.
7. Site map, www.tcha.mus.in.us/images/large/mapcurrent.jpg.
8. Cole, fifth grade, individual interview, October 14, 2004.
9. Calib, fourth grade, individual interview, October 13, 2004.
10. Destiny, fifth grade, individual interview, October 14, 2004.
11. Willey, fourth grade, individual interview, October 13, 2004.
12. Greg, fourth grade, individual interview, October 13, 2004.
13. Destiny, fifth grade, individual interview, October 14, 2004.
14. Harinie, fourth grade, individual interview, October 13, 2004.
15. Greg, fourth grade, individual interview, October 13, 2004.
16. Clifford E. Knapp, "Teaching the 3 R's through the 3 C's: Connecting Curriculum and Community," *Thresholds in Education* 27, 3–4 (2001): 7–9.
17. Patricia K. Coughlin, "Making Field Trips Count: Collaborating for Meaningful Experiences," *Social Studies* 10, 5 (2010): 200–10.
18. Ronald V. Morris, *The Field Trip Book: Study Travel Experience in Social Studies* (Charlotte, NC: Information Age Publishing, 2010).
19. Andrea M. Noel, "Elements of a Winning Field Trip," *Kappa Delta Pi Record* 44, 1 (2007): 42–44.
20. L. Higgins, "School Outings: Fewer Students Get to Go on Field Trips as District Budgets Are Squeezed," *Detroit Free Press*, April 14, 2004.
21. Michael Glassman, "Dewey and Vygotsky: Society, Experience, and Inquiry in Educational Practice," *Educational Researcher* 30, 4 (2001): 3–14.
22. Sylvia S. Martin and Randy L. Seevers, "A Field Trip Planning Guide for Early Childhood Classes," *Preventing School Failure* 47, 4 (2003): 177–80.
23. Sandra T. Martell, "Of Cultural Tools and Kinds of Knowledge: Investigation Field Trip-Based Learning about Art, Culture, and the Environment," *Journal of Museum Education* 33, 2 (2008): 209–20.

24. Kathleen O. Swan, Mark Hofer, and Linda S. Levstik, "Camera! Action! Collaborate with Digital Moviemaking," *Social Studies and the Young Learner* (2007): 17–20.

25. Jane Bolgatz, "Exploring Complexity within a 'Best Story' of US History: Kernels of Inquiry in a Fifth-Grade Class," *International Journal of Social Education* 22, 1 (2007): 1–23.

7

Historical Reenactment at a Living History Site

It was dark and the weather damp with a light breeze, but with the repercussion of a pistol the students lined up to be sold as slaves. By lantern light their master examined them, and their new owner quizzed them on the type of work they performed. The students dreaded the long walk back to slave territory and in an instant an opportunity presented itself where they could bolt to freedom. The students braved the elements, the obstacles of the land, and determined whom they could or could not trust. As the evening progressed the students met many characters who would betray them or help them find their way North on the Underground Railroad.

The staff of Conner Prairie designed their Follow the North Star program to help visitors understand the perils of seeking freedom even in a free state. By taking the role of an enslaved person for about an hour in an outdoor program, visitors learned about different Midwestern points of view on the issue of what to do with escaped slaves. The experience included staff orientation and debriefing of visitors. It also offered an opportunity to determine what dangers the participants might encounter in the coming weeks as they flee to Canada. By directly confronting uncomfortable issues from American history, participants engaged in an experience that is decidedly not celebratory.

INTRODUCTION

Scavenger hunts—we have all been on them. We receive a list of obscure items and a carrying case like a bag, and then we run like crazy from place to place to find all of the required items in the allotted time. But, why do I hate them so much? First of all, they are usually trivial;

they satisfy neither my curiosity nor my need to make sense of the world. Second, they are meaningless. When was I last asked to find a walnut in the shape of Ohio? Adults do not ask these questions of each other.

Finally, I hate scavenger hunts because they are a random, purposeless task created by one person and imposed on another. Even fifth-grade students will follow a scavenger hunt if it has been sold to them well, but as students become older it is more and more difficult to get them to accept a task unless it is their idea.

The key then to the scavenger hunt or to unlocking a historical re-enactment is to find a way for students to accept the task as their own; there must be a purpose or reason for us to accept a task as our own. Therefore, the only acceptable scavenger hunt would be one in which we required the scavenged parts to accomplish a task. We desire to succeed in completing a task in order to satisfy our curiosity or to help create understanding from the world. For the participant in a reenactment it is imperative that the event mirror the real world.

OUTDOOR EDUCATION PROGRAMS

Open-Air History Museum requested ideas to develop new interactive educational programming for elementary students. These programs required direct experiences for students that incorporated reenactment as citizenship building. Students would practice living in a community where they would examine building a community from a historical perspective and talk about issues from civics, citizenship, and what constitutes a civilization while using the example of migration along the National Road (see tables 7.1, 7.2, 7.3, 7.4, and 7.5). Students are traveling on the National Road to their new home in the West when their wagon breaks down near a small town. The students spend their time repairing their wagon, gathering provisions, and meeting local people in this reenactment.

The students engage in multiple decision-making experiences where they must make choices that help them get their wagon repaired. While the students are stranded they take the opportunity to engage in multiple experiences of preserving food to aid them in making their trip west. As students meet people, they find specific tasks or occupations, but they also engage these people in discussion about the issues of the time. This experience covers the National Council for the Social Studies standard of Individuals, Institutions, and Groups.[1]

As a metaphor for community and caring for members of the group, the people would engage in feeding each other. This sharing of meals became incorporated in a reenactment based on the Underground Rail-

Table 7.1:   National Road Outdoor Education Program—Monday

Time	Event
8:30	Introduction: Students are traveling down the road when their wagon breaks down and they need to go to the nearest town to get help. Students learn about life on the National Road. Students gather and find out with whom they will work today.
9:00	Students start with a "Pack a Wagon" activity to determine what they will need as they move west.
9:30	Students meet at their broken wagon where they unload the wagon and meet a peddler who tells about the history of the National Road. They engage in a decision-making opportunity where they decide: Where will we go? What will we do?
10:00	Students carry the wheel pieces into town where they try to get them fixed.
10:30	Restroom break
11:00	Students are directed to the blacksmith shop who can fix the rim Wednesday. The students engage in a decision-making event: can they fix it or do they need to buy a new rim?
11:30	Students check at the carpenter shop but the carpenter is ministering to some sick friends and he is out until Thursday before he can fix the wheel. The students engage in a decision-making experience: can the wheel be fixed or do they need to buy a new wheel?
12:00	Sack lunch/restroom break
12:30	Students decide to go to the inn to find a room for the night. They have a decision-making opportunity when they determine where they will spend the night. At the inn the students do chores to earn their keep. The students wash dishes, wash clothes, sweep, and gather and scramble eggs.
2:00	Restroom break
2:30	Students also go to the store and trade some hides in their wagon for cloth for a straw tick. They sew a straw tick mattress and stuff it with straw.
3:00	Debriefing: Students ask questions and review the experiences they had that day.
3:30	Students learn about the Northwest Ordinance and land claims.
4:00	Depart

road (see tables 7.6, 7.7, 7.8, 7.9, and 7.10). The students keep a watchful eye for strangers in the community who might turn out to be "wolves," a name given to people who would recapture escaped slaves. Even though the students never actually see an escaped slave and their parents would never want them to be a witness to such activity, they do know that the Underground Railroad is transacting business. This ex-

Table 7.2:   National Road Outdoor Education Program—Tuesday

Time	Event
8:30	Introduction: Students gather and find out with whom they will work today.
9:00	National Road map -migration routes to Indiana -counties and towns in 1830s
9:30	Prepare food for trip west -dry beef -dry apples -dry green beans -parch corn -garden -make apple butter -wash dishes
10:30	Restroom
11:00	Prepare food for trip west -dry beef -dry apples -dry green beans -parch corn -garden -make apple butter -wash dishes
11:30	Smoking: Pro and con views.
12:00	Sack lunch/restroom break
12:30	Fire: bucket brigade.
1:00	Grease for wheels: What will they trade for it?
1:30	Leather for harnesses: What will they trade for it?
2:00	Restroom break
2:30	Debriefing: Students ask questions and review the experiences they had that day.
3:00	Economics and currency/buying power and trade
3:30	Depart

perience covers the NCSS standard of Authority and Governance when students encounter a variety of abolition ideas and multiple ideas and attitudes from the time.[2]

Students learn what children might have been asked to do to help on

Table 7.3: National Road Outdoor Education Program—Wednesday

Time	Event
8:30	Introduction: Students gather and find out with whom they will work today.
9:00	Mammoth Internal Improvement Act map
9:30	Cut wheat
10:00	Thrash wheat
10:30	Restroom
11:00	Grind wheat
11:30	Build fire
12:00	Sack lunch/restroom break
12:30	Mix bread
1:00	Cook bread
1:30	Wash dishes
2:00	Restroom break
2:30	Immigrants: Their story; anti-immigrant feeling.
3:00	Debriefing: Students ask questions and review the experiences they had that day.
3:30	Depart

Table 7.4: National Road Outdoor Education Program—Thursday

Time	Event
8:30	Introduction: Students gather and find out with whom they will work today.
9:00	Pioneer songs and music
9:30	Carpenter shop to complete wheel: His story of creating specialty products for customers using tools and woods.
10:00	Shave spokes Chisel wood
10:30	Restroom
11:00	Make wagon jack Plane wood Sand wood Seal wood
11:30	Drill holes Saw wood Draw knife and shaving horse
12:00	Sack lunch/restroom break
12:30	Education: Talk to the school master.
1:00	Politics: Talk to a candidate.
1:30	Election: Talk to the doctor about the election.
2:00	Restroom break
2:30	State of women: Talk to a women in the town.
3:00	Learn square dance
3:30	Debriefing: Students ask questions and review the experiences they had that day.
4:00	Depart

Table 7.5: National Road Outdoor Education Program—Friday

Time	Event
8:30	Introduction: Students gather and find out with whom they will work today.
9:00	Blacksmith shop: How he does specialty work for clients, welding and riming a wagon wheel.
9:30	Saw and drill antler buttons
10:00	File Rivet Bring water Bring coal Work bellows Cut nail Seal iron
10:30	Restroom break
11:00	Continue
11:30	Jack wagon and replace the wheel
12:00	Sack lunch/restroom break
12:30	Wagon ride
1:00	Square dance
1:30	Load wagon
2:00	Restroom break
2:30	Debriefing: Students ask questions and review the experiences they had that day.
3:00	Depart

the Underground Railroad. The students also try a variety of experiences an escaped slave might use to flee to freedom, from rubbing onions on their feet to trying on a shipping crate for size. They make clothes a slave could change into and prepare food a slave might carry on the trip. They also acquire provisions and solicit money for purchasing shoes for escaped slaves between pioneer games.

Each reenactment experience engages in real work for the benefit of the community. In the Fall Creek Massacre reenactment, students must take on the role of members of the courtroom (see tables 7.11, 7.12, 7.13, 7.14, and 7.15). In this program the students learn about the temperance movement, the pioneer justice system, and Native American–settler relations. Students examine conflicting accounts and alternative interpretations of events as they try to sort through the events. The students look at the presence of alcohol abuse in frontier society and deal with issues of hate and prejudice. Students work with the conflicts that result in a society based on violence and revenge. This experience covers the NCSS

Table 7.6:   Underground Railroad Outdoor Education Program—Monday

Time	Event
8:30	Introduction: This week students will learn how some Quaker children in the town of Newport acted as agents for the Underground Railroad. They will gather and meet the people with whom they will work today.
9:00	The first person students meet is a prolaw Quaker who believes that they should work on separating themselves from the world and not interact in it.
9:30	Students are sent on an errand to collect money from mother's friends in the village. They find out what motivates people to give money to this cause.
10:00	Mother captures them and has them make dipper gourds.
10:30	Restroom break
11:00	Students walk around the town looking for wolves (slave catchers) after finding out they have a very important job to do.
11:30	Students look for hiding places around the town.
12:00	Sack lunch/restroom break
12:30	Students find a man who is prejudiced and find that this is the majority view at this time.
1:00	Mother has the students sewing clothes for escaped slaves: shirt petticoat knit scarf.
1:30	Mother has the students take the money to store and buy shoes, but the storekeeper is suspicious.
2:00	Restroom break
2:30	Debriefing: Students ask questions and review the experiences they had that day.
3:00	Students create a map that shows important places on the Underground Railroad in Indiana.
3:30	Students view a segment from the *Traces and Trails* DVD.
4:00	Depart

standard of Time, Continuity, and Change.[3] Participants spend significant time on law related education, especially learning about the jury, the grand jury, and a trial by jury. Equal time is spent on examining both sides of the case.

A reenactment experience integrates multiple generations into the learning environment. This experience covers the NCSS standard of Individual Growth and Identity.[4] In the Cane Ridge reenactment, students work in partnership with parents and grandparents (see tables 7.16, 7.17, 7.18, 7.19, and 7.20). Students learn about Protestant social reform in the context of the western Great Awakening while encountering ideas from

Table 7.7: Underground Railroad Outdoor Education Program—Tuesday

Time	Event
8:30	Introduction: Students meet the people they will work with today.
9:00	Students meet newspaper editor Arnold Buffington, who prints an abolitionist newspaper.
9:30	Students are told to get water and leave it in the barn.
10:00	Students meet a proslavery minister who tells them about how the Bible justifies slavery.
10:30	Restroom break
11:00	Students need to call for the doctor to come with them, but then they cannot see the escaped slave. The doctor tells of escaped slaves he has treated in the past. That way they can tell the truth if asked.
11:30	Students visit the blacksmith, who is making leg irons and chains and he tells about the things he has made for masters transporting slaves.
12:00	Sack lunch/restroom break
12:30	Students meet the carpenter, who is making shipping crates. The students try them on for size.
1:00	Students pick up the empty water bucket at barn.
1:30	Debriefing: Students ask questions and review the experiences they had that day.
2:00	Restroom break
2:30	Students see clips of the *Madison* DVD.
3:00	Students make an Indiana map showing free black populations in Indiana.
3:30	Students play the *Escape to Freedom* CD.
4:00	Depart

many different religious groups. Students meet a variety of people who practice many different religious traditions including those of the Native Americans, religions such as that of the Shakers that are no longer popular, and atheism.

While students do not actually participate in religious services, they do talk about the ideas that both divide and unite these people. Students also talk about cultural transition ceremonies, such as weddings and funerals. Students help the soon-to-be-married couple make furniture for their new home, sew their initials on their linens, and prepare the wedding dinner. The entire experience culminates in a wedding.

Students need the opportunity to develop autonomy in mastering skills leading to individual growth. In the Flatboat reenactment students get to cultivate new skills (see tables 7.21, 7.22, 7.23, 7.24, and 7.25). Students come off the river to establish their new home in the wilderness; at the

Table 7.8: Underground Railroad Outdoor Education Program—Wednesday

Time	Event
8:30	Introduction: Students meet the people they will work with today.
9:00	The students build fires, make food, wash dishes, and sample: corn oysters ham omelet salad
9:30	The students take food to the barn in a basket and leave it there.
10:00	At the barn students learn some songs that they sing: "Swing Low Sweet Chariot" "Go Down Moses"
10:30	Restroom break
11:00	Students meet a free black conductor who tells her story.
11:30	A wolf comes to the door, but after telling his story he goes away without entering since he has no warrant.
12:00	Sack lunch/restroom break
12:30	Students meet a member of the American Colonization Society, who tells them about the work of the group.
1:00	Students pick up the empty basket from the barn.
1:30	A town member meets students to tell them why he would like to be a wolf.
2:00	Restroom break
2:30	Debriefing: Students ask questions and review the experiences they had that day.
3:00	Students look at a slave ship drawing and model how small that space would be for them.
3:30	Students look at newspaper ads for escaped slaves in Indiana.
4:00	Depart

same time they need to gather goods they can take down river to New Orleans to sell for cash. This experience covers the NCSS standard of Production, Consumption, and Distribution.[5] The students meet many different people who travel along the river and expose them to the issues of the day. The students both work on their new home and repair their boat; at the same time they work with textiles in order to repair their clothing.

Students engage in economic decision making when they choose what to take and what to sell to get the best return on their investment. Along with these choices the students engage in food preservation and preparation to guarantee a food supply on their journey. Students also learn basic navigation skills so that they can find their way down the river and make their way back over land as they walk back home.

Table 7.9:   Underground Railroad Outdoor Education Program—Thursday

Time	Event
8:30	Introduction: Students meet the people they will work with today.
9:00	The mother tells the students more about the Underground Railroad. Hiding two girls in a bed and how they started to laugh Candles in windows "Friend of a Friend" Star chart Map of area where to find help
9:30	Students build fire, make traveling food, wash dishes, sample, and drop this food inside the barn: Baked sweet potatoes Baked corn pone
10:00	Students borrow a horse and a wagon.
10:30	Restroom break
11:00	Students load boxes on the wagon leaving a space large enough for a person between the boxes. Students try both the boxes and the space as the wagon goes down the road.
11:30	Students disguise themselves and move from one end of town to the other, trying not to be seen.
12:00	Sack lunch/restroom break
12:30	In groups of threes, two students try to get the third student from place to place without being seen.
1:00	A slave catcher intersects the students, accuses them of acting peculiar, and wonders if they are hiding slaves.
1:30	Students try rubbing onions and pepper on their feet and shoes.
2:00	Restroom break
2:30	Debriefing: Students ask questions and review the experiences they had that day.
3:00	Students read excerpts of *Friendly Mission*, a primary source diary of some Abolitionist English Quakers.
3:30	The students look at photos of former enslaved people.
4:00	Depart

A WORD OF CAUTION

Four areas of caution should be observed in creating reenactment experiences. First, the lack or limits of either preparation or debriefing deprives the participant of required information necessary to make meaning from the experience. The lack of primary source material is particularly limiting. Second, the culture of the reenactors may perpetuate values, myths,

Table 7.10:   Underground Railroad Outdoor Education Program—Friday

Time	Event
8:30	Introduction: They meet the people they will work with today.
9:00	Students meet a slave owner, and he tells about his life.
9:30	Students go through town to raise money for free blacks in Canada from Father's Friends.
10:00	Students play pioneer games including: Tug of war Hoop and stick Stilts Jump rope Hopscotch Andy over
10:30	Restroom break
11:00	Pioneer games
12:00	Sack lunch/restroom break
12:30	Students act out the Grand Jury proceedings against Levi Coffin.
1:00	Debriefing: Students ask questions and review the experiences they had that day.
2:00	Restroom break
2:30	Students make a time line showing events leading to the abolition of slavery.
3:00	Depart

Table 7.11:   Fall Creek Massacre Outdoor Education Program—Monday

Time	Event
8:30	Introduction: Students pretend they live in the area and gather crops for market. In this Program, students will learn about the temperance movement, the pioneer justice system, and Native American relations. Students gather and find out with whom they will work today.
9:00	Farmer: Tells of Native American atrocities when his father was young.
9:30	Pick corn
10:00	Native camp: Tells of settler atrocities when his father was young.
10:30	Restroom break
11:00	Inn prejudice: Tells of prejudice toward Native Americans.
11:30	Corn husking bee: Tells of noble savage, falling in love with a Native American princess, and other Native American myths.
12:00	Sack lunch/restroom break
12:30	Store: Talks about treaty conditions, land and alcohol, selling alcohol, and cheating Native Americans in trade.
1:00	Hull corn
1:30	Debriefing: Students ask questions and review the experiences they had that day.
2:00	Restroom break
2:30	Constitution simulation
3:00	Trial-by-jury simulation
3:30	Depart

Table 7.12:   Fall Creek Massacre Outdoor Education Program—Tuesday

Time	Event
8:30	Introduction: Students gather and find out with whom they will work today.
9:00	Grind corn: How to make money from milling and water power.
9:30	Inn drunk: Alcohol abuse on the frontier.
10:00	Corn cob darts
10:30	Restroom break
11:00	Turkey shoot: Skill and recreation on the frontier.
11:30	Corn husk figures
12:00	Sack lunch/restroom break
12:30	Temperance: Organizing efforts to change society as moral improvement.
1:00	Carpenter making coffins: How he fits into the local economy.
1:30	Debriefing: Students ask questions and review the experiences they had that day.
2:00	Indiana Native Americans' map
2:30	Native American speeches
3:00	Depart

Table 7.13:   Fall Creek Massacre Outdoor Education Program—Wednesday

Time	Event
8:30	Introduction: Students gather and find out with whom they will work today.
9:00	Native Village: Events at the scene of the crime.
9:30	Harvest barley.
10:00	Interview witness to the crime.
10:30	Restroom break
11:00	Plant grapes.
11:30	Press apple cider.
12:00	Sack lunch/restroom break
12:30	Interview accused: His account of why he was within his right to kill an Indian.
1:00	Debriefing: Students ask questions and review the experiences they had that day.
1:30	Pro view: Students summarize one side of the story.
2:00	Restroom break
2:30	Con view: Students summarize another side of the story.
3:00	Duret Diary
3:30	Depart

Table 7.14: Fall Creek Massacre Outdoor Education Program—Thursday

Time	Event
8:30	Introduction: Students gather and find out with whom they will work today.
9:00	Grand jury: Selecting a grand jury of students and their job.
9:30	Warrant: Judge and Sheriff issue warrants—pioneer justice, jails, and courts.
10:00	Sheriff and deputies: Sheriff swears in student deputies.
10:30	Restroom break
11:00	Sheriff arrest and charges: Sheriff and deputies arrest and charge the men.
11:30	Jury trial #1 – Jury selected from students and prepared.
12:00	Sack lunch/restroom break
12:30	Jury trial #2 – Court trial
1:00	Jury trial #3 – Jury deliberations
1:30	Debriefing: Students ask questions and review the experiences they had that day.
2:00	Restroom break
2:30	Native people today
3:00	Depart

Table 7.15: Fall Creek Massacre Outdoor Education Program—Friday

Time	Event
8:30	Introduction: Students gather and find out with whom they will work today.
9:00	Interview survivor: How they saw the events.
9:30	Sentencing: Judge and accused.
10:00	Hanging: Follow accused in wagon—stop at the edge of town where the hanging is described.
10:30	Restroom break
11:00	Native village: Indian story after the trial.
11:30	Funerals: Pioneer religion and mourning.
12:00	Sack lunch/restroom break
12:30	Debriefing: Students ask questions and review the experiences they had that day.
1:00	Pro view: Was justice served?
1:30	Con view: Was justice served?
2:00	Restroom break
2:30	Native people and civic rights
3:00	Map of Native American expulsions from Indiana
3:30	Depart

Table 7.16: Cane Ridge Meeting Outdoor Education Program—Monday

Time	Event
8:30	Introduction: Students live in area, a couple is getting married, and a camp meeting is about to begin. The students learn that this week they will determine the religious views of people who came to America. Students gather and find out with whom they will work today.
9:00	Announcement of wedding: Students meet the two individuals, who each do a first-person presentation on gender roles, expectations, hopes, and dreams. Then they meet, talk to each other, and propose.
9:30	Moravian: The students meet a Moravian woman, mother of the engaged girl, and she tells them about her life and beliefs.
10:00	She invites students to help her two daughters make food for the approaching Love Feast. Students get to work in each group. Group I: Coffee Students build a fire, roast, grind, and brew coffee, wash the dishes, and sample the products. Group II: Rolls The students build a fire, mix, bake the rolls, wash the dishes, and sample the products. Group III: Moravian ginger cookies Students build a fire, mix, bake, wash the dishes, and sample the products.
10:30	Restroom break
11:00	Sweedenborgian: A missionary wanders into the students asking for directions. He tells them about his past and what he believes.
11:30	The Moravian mother invites the group of students to plant apple seeds on her farm.
12:00	Sack lunch/restroom break
12:30	A member of the Church of Brethren inquires as to where he can find German-speaking people. He describes his life and beliefs.
1:00	Invite guests to wedding: Students travel around the 1836 village inviting the townspeople to the wedding.
1:30	A member of the Lutheran church is looking for the Brethren so he can preach to the same group of people. He talks about his life and beliefs.
2:00	Restroom break
2:30	Debriefing: Students ask questions and review the experiences they had that day.
3:00	At this point students go out of character to create a map of Europe showing where different religions originated.
3:30	The students follow up this experience by creating a map of America where religions started and were active.
4:00	Depart

Table 7.17: Cane Ridge Meeting Outdoor Education Program—Tuesday

Time	Event
8:30	Introduction: Students gather and find out with whom they will work today.
9:00	Students meet a Campbellite, who is helping set up a camp meeting and they find out about his past and beliefs.
9:30	The Moravian mother invites students to help her sew pillow cases for the couple that is engaged to be married.
10:00	The Methodist circuit rider arrives for the camp meeting and invites students to form a Sunday school.
10:30	Restroom break
11:00	A Shaker inquires about the camp meeting and tells her story.
11:30	The Moravian mother sends students to the carpenter to find out if he has the chest for the new family done and how he is coming on building benches for the camp meeting. An Owenite is traveling looking for rocks and minerals, and he talks about his life and beliefs.
12:00	Sack lunch/restroom break
12:30	The carpenter throws the Owenite out of his shop and invites the students to help him work on the benches and chest. Students go to stations where they: compare wood types measure saw drill peg chisel plane file.
1:00	Debriefing: Students ask questions and review the experiences they had that day.
1:30	Students watch two video clips from *The Shadow of Hate* video and talk about religious toleration in America.
2:00	Restroom break
2:30	Students create a timeline of wedding practices to determine when ideas about marriage appeared in popular culture.
3:00	Depart

legends, and stories that they come to believe is really the way the past was. Since it is part of the reenactor culture, it is perpetuated and sustained by members of the culture.[6] The third idea is *presentism*, or the idea that because our life today is like this, those people long ago must have felt the same way. The motivations, values, and thoughts might have been very different or subtly different from those of twenty-first-century Americans.

Table 7.18: Cane Ridge Meeting Outdoor Education Program—Wednesday

Time	Event
8:30	Introduction: Students gather and find out with whom they will work today.
9:00	Students meet a Jewish pack peddler who talks about his life and beliefs.
9:30	The carpenter invites students to help make the speakers' box for the camp meeting. Students go to stations where they: compare wood types measure saw drill peg chisel plane file.
10:00	A Quaker, father of the groom, comes by to ask the carpenter to make a bed for the new couple as a surprise gift. He tells about his life and beliefs.
10:30	Restroom break
11:00	The carpenter invites students to help create the bed. Students go to stations where they: compare wood types measure saw drill peg chisel plane file.
11:30	A Catholic is heading for St. Meinrad to attend school. He talks about his life and beliefs.
12:00	Sack lunch/restroom break
12:30	A free black drover talks about his life and beliefs.
1:00	The Moravian mother invites students to make pillows for the engaged couple and the students sew and stuff pillows.
1:30	An Episcopalian priest is traveling to set up a new parish. He talks about his life and beliefs.
2:00	Restroom break
2:30	Students create a graphic organizer to trace the roots of religion. This looks like a family tree with groups splintering and merging.
3:00	Students compare Hitchcock and Shaker chairs.
3:30	Debriefing: Students ask questions and review the experiences they had that day.
4:00	Depart

Table 7.19:   Cane Ridge Meeting Outdoor Education Program—Thursday

Time	Event
8:30	Introduction: Students gather and find out with whom they will work today.
9:00	Students meet a Baptist at the river looking for a place to baptize converts after the camp meeting. He talks about his life and beliefs.
9:30	Students decide to cook a lunch they can take to the camp meeting. Students work in all of the groups to build a fire, wash dishes, hull nuts and churn butter, and make: hoe cake bacon fried apple pies apple sauce.
10:00	They meet a Lenape who has returned to visit the place where he was born. He talks about his life in the west and his beliefs.
10:30	Restroom break
11:00	Students work in all of the groups to build a fire, wash dishes, hull nuts and churn butter, and make: hoe cake bacon fried apple pies apple sauce.
11:30	A Presbyterian is trying to sell land. He talks about his life and beliefs.
12:00	Sack lunch/restroom break
12:30	The Camp Meeting occurs.
1:00	Students work to make quilt squares for the new family. They cut old clothes into pieces and sew two pieces together.
1:30	Students also sew sheets for the new family.
2:00	Restroom break
2:30	Debriefing: Students ask questions and review the experiences they had that day.
3:00	Students work with primary sources from Father Rapp's New Harmony to determine what life was like for people on the banks on the Wabash.
3:30	Students create a graphic organizer showing where the Rapp beliefs derived.
4:00	Depart

Finally, there is Tellyism, which means that in retrospect the participant sees that A happened, therefore they think events B and C must have caused A to occur. These may be coincidental or tangential rather than causational relationships. Reenactors who get caught in these traps need significant in-service working with primary sources and scholars to examine issues of the time period.

Table 7.20: Cane Ridge Meeting Outdoor Education Program—Friday

Time	Event
8:30	Introduction: Students gather and find out with whom they will work today.
9:00	Students decide to cook food for the wedding meal. All of them work in all of the groups to build a fire, wash dishes, bake, and sample: gingerbread marble cake fruit glaze pound cake lemon cake lemon glaze.
10:30	Restroom break
11:00	Students continue to cook the wedding meal.
12:00	Sack lunch/restroom break
12:30	Wedding decision making: What groups could be asked to officiate? Which group should be asked to officiate at the wedding and why? Decision making: Can we have music? Decision making: Can we square dance?
1:00	Contra dance
1:30	Students play pioneer games including: Noah's Ark Sticks Dominos Checkers Hoop and stick Stilts Jacob's Ladder
2:00	Restroom break
2:30	Debriefing: Students ask questions and review the experiences they had that day.
3:00	Students get to work with Owen primary sources to find out about life in a secular society with Freethinkers.
3:30	Students get to create a circuit map showing where a pastor would travel in the course of a year.
4:00	Depart

FOUNDATIONS

Inquiry is a form of seeking understanding about the nature of the world through gathering and testing information. Educators have promoted the method of inquiry as a desirable means of teaching and learning. Johnson (2010) and Sunal and Haas (2010) define inquiry as

Table 7.21:   Flatboat Outdoor Education Program—Monday

Time	Event
8:30	Introduction: Students came down the river on this boat, and they are living on it until they build their cabin. They need to take a load of produce down to New Orleans. In this program students will learn about life on the Ohio River. Students gather and find out with whom they will work today.
9:00	Students paint the boat with linseed oil to keep it water tight on their voyage down the river.
9:30	Students harvest flax to get ready for winter.
10:00	The carpenter makes a new sweep so they can take the flat boat down river in the fall with all of their produce.
10:30	Restroom break
11:00	A traveler passes by interested in talking about prison reform.
11:30	Students ret the flax to get ready for winter.
12:00	Sack lunch/restroom break
12:30	A traveler passes them with news of the Alamo and Goliad. The story of the Texas Revolution does not have a happy ending yet.
1:00	Students sheer sheep.
1:30	Students wash wool to prepare for winter.
2:00	Restroom break
2:30	Debriefing: Students ask questions and review the experiences they had that day.
3:00	Students perform a simulation to pack a flat boat.
3:30	Students make river and town maps of their journey.
4:00	Depart

a form of research to answer questions about social studies problems.[7] By using a problem-solving approach students engage to become active learners. The key to elementary social studies is encouraging the citizen to make good decisions that positively impact the community. Through the connections the students make with the community, they construct meaningful ways to achieve proficiency in social studies standards.

The definition of the problem allows people to identify what it is that they seek rather than remaining in doubt and uncertainty. When people define a problem, many people feel motivated to seek a solution to that problem. Organic problems may include finding esteem for self, the esteem of others, food, shelter, and mental or physical sensory stimulation. These problems may include either physical or cognitive dissonances. The resolution of the problem may be a form of stress reduction or it may take the form of a pleasurable pursuit. The problem could be an immediate need or a continuing need.

Table 7.22:   Flatboat Outdoor Education Program—Tuesday

Time	Event
8:30	Introduction: Students gather and find out with whom they will work today.
9:00	Students make tar and tar the boat.
9:30	Students go to the store and ask the terms for taking produce for the storekeeper to New Orleans.
10:00	Students wash clothing after their trip on the flat boat.
10:30	Restroom break
11:00	Students use the flax break to process the fiber.
11:30	Students use the flax hackles to comb the fibers.
12:00	Sack lunch/restroom break
12:30	Students go to the still house to talk about distilling corn into whiskey as a better selling product in the New Orleans trade.
1:00	Students spin flax into thread.
1:30	Students meet a man who is on poor relief.
2:00	Restroom break
2:30	He invites them to come and sing river songs with him, including: "Shawnee Town" "Dance Boatman Dance" "Erie Canal"
3:00	Debriefing: Students ask questions and review the experiences they had that day.
3:30	Students create a map of Indiana counties from this time.
4:00	Depart

As students look at problems to be solved in museums or through educational programming, they need to examine problems in society. These real issues give museums and educational programming relevance and take the problem from the glass case and into the life of the participant. Problems such as equity, justice, equal access, discrimination, poverty, and education are problems that each generation examine and develop public policy to redress in their own time. These problems are called "persistent issues." A problem in society, or a persistent issue, would be a reoccurring issue that emerges with each generation when society revisits the problem to address and resolve the problem in the context of their time. These issues, located at the heart of the experience, launch participants into discussions of their beliefs.

Since the students or visitors only have a small amount of time to interact at a site, it is important to consider what knowledge the staff wishes to impart that has the most social worth. If the guest comes to a site and we have an opportunity to dip candles or talk about immigration, which

Table 7.23:   Flatboat Outdoor Education Program—Wednesday

Time	Event
8:30	Introduction: Students gather and find with whom they will work today.
9:00	Students pick wool.
9:30	Students card wool.
10:00	Students spin wool into thread.
10:30	Restroom break
11:00	Students dye wool.
11:30	Students weave wool into cloth for winter clothes.
12:00	Sack lunch/restroom break
12:30	The militia musters and drills as part of the responsibilities for citizens in their new home.
1:00	Students go to the potter to get containers for food storage.
1:30	Debriefing: Students ask questions and review the experiences they had that day.
2:00	Restroom break
2:30	Students make drawings of different types of river transportation for a mural.
3:00	Students learn about world events in Europe, South America, Asia, and Africa.
3:30	Students go into the visitor's center and listen to a story about the frontier.
4:00	Depart.

topic has more value to our society? The issue of immigration has direct implications to public policy questions encountered by Americans in the present.

While it is a cool and groovy activity by itself, dipping candles has little relevance to modern Americans until is placed in context with issues of energy production and consumption or economics. The knowledge of most social worth comes from the interpretation of the experience coupled with new understandings, insights, and understandings. The ideal interaction would be to connect a direct experience with comprehensive examination of questions, concepts, facts, and generalizations that support the participatory experience.

The advantage of connecting history and drama is the development of a sense of community and open-ended experiences. Many people have written about the interaction between drama and playfulness.[8] People do engage in historical reenactment because it is fun. They get to play while they have new adventures, experiences, and insights, and they learn from each of these. They get to use their imagination to recreate a place and time that they cannot directly experience except through their mind's eye. Similarly, the reenactment participant must engage in creativity to

Table 7.24: Flatboat Outdoor Education Program—Thursday

Time	Event
8:30	Introduction: Students gather and find out with whom they will work today.
9:00	Students help a man burn brick in the village to construct their fireplace.
9:30	Students meet another river traveler interested in mental health reform.
10:00	Students meet a seminary student traveling for an education at Transylvania University.
10:30	Restroom break
11:00	Students climb on the flatboat and prepare for their voyage down to New Orleans. Students learn to: -tie knots -use a compass - navigate using charts and maps - use observation and steer to look for snags and shallows.
11:30	After washing clothes, students find they are almost out of soap so they make soap
12:00	Sack lunch/restroom break
12:30	Students preserve food, drying green beans into "leather breeches" (dehydrated bean pods with the beans inside).
1:00	Students preserve food for the trip by making apple butter and sealing it in crocks.
1:30	Students preserve food by turning milk into cheese.
2:00	Restroom break
2:30	Debriefing: Students ask questions and review the experiences they had that day.
3:00	Students learn about national events.
3:30	Depart

reconstruct what life must have been like, what life could have been like, what life might not have been like, and what life most likely was not like.

The reenactment participant creates a reality based experience dependent upon critically examining artifacts, clothing, and experiences. Artifacts representing a variety of cultures figure prominently in play and even older students need models to develop understanding.[9] When learning new skills students need artifacts to construct consistent internal models.

Unlike a theater experience where an audience watches events on stage but does not interact with them, the participants do not remain behind an invisible glass wall in a reenactment. At a reenactment participants expect to interact with multiple other characters.[10] The participants interact with the reenactment through a visit to the site, and they play along when they encounter the script or the experience similar to playing a live action videogame. Continuing with this analogy of a game the experience should be

Table 7.25: Flatboat Outdoor Education Program—Friday

Time	Event
8:30	Introduction: Students gather and find out with whom they will work today.
9:00	Students help a man make charcoal so they can cook on the boat or on the shore.
9:30	Students bake bread for the trip.
10:00	Students load the flatboat for their voyage down the river.
10:30	Restroom break
11:00	Students cook shortbread for the trip.
11:30	Students cook cornbread for the trip.
12:00	Sack lunch/restroom break
12:30	Students make shingles they can use on their home.
1:00	Students whittle pegs they can use in their home.
1:30	Students celebrate their departure with play party games such as Oh Johnny.
2:00	Restroom break
2:30	Students celebrate their departure with pioneer games such as stilts and corn cob checkers.
3:00	Debriefing: Students ask questions and review the experiences they had that day.
3:30	Students determine what events occurred in the state at this time.
4:00	Depart

nonlinear. The participants interact with some features of the reenactment that they select but not necessarily all of them.

Historical reenactment happens both in the classroom and in extracurricular experiences.[11] Other reenactment programs, sometimes called living history, incorporate first-person presentations to create immersion programs.[12] Students explore an interdisciplinary curriculum while meeting national social studies standards and investigating through inquiry projects. Many of these reenactment programs require support resources for teachers and first person historical presentations that last up to a week for the students.

Furthermore, the participants may interact with events in whatever order they elect. The reenactment moves away from the predestination of a script and allows for the multiple possibilities of the participant to exercise his or her free will. The participants then take a role and engage in decision-making across the events of the experience.

This process is similar to the old *Choose Your Own Adventure* books.[13] The creators of the reenactment need to determine to what extent the reenactment responds to the choices of the participants. This nonsequential engagement allows for individual differences and differing maturational needs. Real choice allows for participants to have an element of power over the reenactment experience.

CONCLUSIONS

Thus the principles of reenactment experience incorporate intellectual, social, and emotional aspects. The intellectual aspect of reenactment includes power, curiosity, and educative function. The participant needs the power to shape his or her own questions, and the reenactment experience needs to incite curiosity and the desire to explore more. Finally, the reenactment must have some sort of educational function. If the reenactment were completely free, play reenactors would just go to the pool or the playground rather than to a museum, historical society, or living history site.

The reenactment has a definite social component. A reenactment rejects an individual experience over a significant common experience with a family or group. People share common experiences, ideas, and values when they invest time with each other. There is intergroup interaction, and of course, the element of play needs to be present so that the event is felicitous. Playfully engaging with one another for a sustained interval allows for interaction and allows the reenactor to enjoy the group experience.

The reenactment satisfies an emotional requirement. Participants find fulfillment when they engage with social issues and community problems; younger participants particularly like to have happy endings. Reenactors find satisfaction when they engage in three types of experience including civic, deliberative, and hands-on activities to make meaning of their event. Finally, regardless of their age the reenactor accesses the event at their own emotional level. The emotional satisfaction of reenacting keeps reenactors returning to similar events multiple times across multiple years.

Teachers and students find content and situations for historical reenactment provided by the interaction of several elements. Historical reenactment depends upon the process of inquiry to guide the exploration and investigation of events and situations imposed by the conditions of the reenactment. Persistent issues are natural fodder for historical reenactments when they connect people to relevant problems from the past that still have implications for the present. Historical reenactment presents an opportunity to work with knowledge of the most social worth to highlight important concepts and ideas. History and drama work together to provide the content for the historical reenactment. Reenactment is both open ended and interactive.

NOTES

1. National Council for the Social Studies, *National Standards for Social Studies Teachers* (Washington, DC: National Council for the Social Studies, 2002).

2. National Council for the Social Studies, *National Standards for Social Studies Teachers*.

3. National Council for the Social Studies, *National Standards for Social Studies Teachers*.

4. National Council for the Social Studies, *National Standards for Social Studies Teachers*.

5. National Council for the Social Studies, *National Standards for Social Studies Teachers*.

6. Kenneth Yellis, "Cueing the Visitor: The Museum Theater and the Visitor Performance," *Curator* 53, 1 (2010): 87–103; Kenneth Yellis, "Fred Wilson, PTSD, and Me: Reflections on the History Wars," *Curator* 52, 4 (2009): 333–48.

7. Andrew P. Johnson, *Making Connections in Elementary and Middle School Social Studies*, 2nd ed. (Thousand Oaks, CA: Sage, 2010); Cynthia S. Sunal and Mary E. Haas, *Social Studies for the Elementary and Middle Grades: A Constructivist Approach* (Boston: Allyn & Bacon, 2010).

8. Timothy Crumrin, L. Bunch, and William Munn, "David Thelen's 'Learning from the Past': A Conversation with the IMH," *Indiana Magazine of History* 49, 2 (2003): 165–71; David Thelen, "Learning from the Past: Individual Experience and Reenactment," *Indiana Magazine of History* 49, 2 (2003): 155–64.

9. Liane Brouillette, "Bringing Jazz Back to Its Roots: Inner City Students Explore Their Musical Heritage," *Teaching Artist Journal* 4, 1 (2006): 39–46; Gina Lewis, "Putting the Arts into the Classroom: Active Learning through Drama," *Understanding Our Gifted* 18, 3 (2006): 23–24; Francis Prendiville and Nigel Toye, *Speaking and Listening through Drama 7–11*.(Thousand Oaks, CA: Paul Chapman, 2007).

10. Peggy M. Elgas, Jo-Anne Prendeville, Sally Moomaw, and Richard R. Kretschmer, "Early Childhood Classroom Setup," *Child Care Information Exchange* 143 (2002): 17–20; Stella Vosniadou, Irina Skopeliti, and Kalliopi Ikospentaki, "Reconsidering the Role of Artifacts in Reasoning: Children's Understanding of the Globe as a Model of the Earth," *Learning and Instruction* 15, 4 (2005): 333–51.

11. Daniel A. Kelin, II, "To Feel the Fear of It: Engaging Young People in Social Education," *Talking Points* 14, 1 (2002): 10–14; Barbara J. Michels and Deborah K. Maxwell, "An After-School Program for Interpreting Local History," *Tech Trends: Linking Research and Practice to Improve Learning* 50, 2 (2006): 62–66.

12. David L. Buckner, Pamela U. Brown, and John Curry, "The Pleasant Valley School: A Living History Project," *Social Education* 74, 2 (2010): 65–66; Sharon Coatney and Rachel Smalley, "Inquiry and Living History, Part II," *School Library Media Activities Monthly* 22, 5 (2006): 28–31; Sharon Coatney and Rachel Smalley, "Inquiry and Living History, Part I," *School Library Media Activities Monthly* 22, 4 (2005): 24–27; Barbara C. Cruz and Shalini A. Murthy, "Breathing Life into History: Using Role-playing to Engage Students," *Social Studies and the Young Learner* 19, 1 (2006): 4–8; Carol Peterson, *Jump Back in Time: A Living History Resource* (Portsmouth, NH: Teacher Ideas Press, 2004).

13. R. A. Montgomery, *Choose Your Own Adventure Books, Box Set #1–4: The Abominable Snowman/Journey under the Sea/Space and Beyond/The Lost Jewels of Nabooti* (Waitsfield, VT: Chooseco, 2006).

8

Extracurricular Social Studies at the Conner Prairie Interpretive Park

"May I work tomorrow?" At the end of the day and before the youths meet their parents, they often raise this hopeful question. Parents help their talented child by encouraging their child to find a supportive community and engage with that community through extracurricular activities.

Teachers can also learn from a successful extracurricular program when they discover how they can build similar service-learning programs that mentor talented students.[1] Students learn academic content and skills and provide a real service for a real audience, which is an important part of a service-learning program. Gifted students find community through sorting themselves into extracurricular programs offered by cultural institutions. Conner Prairie Interpretive Park is a cultural institution that encourages and supports talented students as they participate in an extracurricular program.

Ten- to eighteen-year-old youths "apply for jobs" as youth volunteers at Conner Prairie Interpretive Park, where they either work to help adult or student visitors experience the site. The students work at least two days per month; because returning youths have places reserved for them the following year, it is considered an honor to fill one of the few positions available each year. Gifted youths enjoy learning about the past and working with visitors; they consider themselves and their jobs equal to those of the paid adult interpreters. The youth volunteers establish a sense of community in which they enjoy a common purpose, feel safe and comfortable, and share responsibility.

With a professional staff of approximately 100 and more than 250 part-time interpreters contributing to the operation of the private nonprofit museum, Conner Prairie Interpretive Park is located in the suburban community adjacent to a city. Conner Prairie Interpretive Park staff members educate the general public by showing buildings, artifacts, and people with interrelated context while maintaining stringent standards of accuracy and historical authenticity.

Because of these high standards, visitors receive some surprises when they discover unanticipated truths about history. Conner Prairie Interpretive Park presents a collection of reenactors representing a variety of social classes, including the average citizen rather than just the extremes, who are engaged in seasonal activities. These are not cut off from the rest of the nation; the pioneer village inn functions as a foil to show connections to the outside world.

At Conner Prairie Interpretive Park each area is set in a different time period, and the interpretation changes between areas. The museum provides interpretation through four areas including the following: Lenape Indian Camp, Conner House, Pioneer Village, and Civil War Journey. The Past Port area allows visitors to engage in pioneer skills, games, and activities.

The docents interpret the Conner House in third person, use first person to interpret the Pioneer Village, and use a mixture of first and third person in the Lenape Indian Camp and the Civil War Journey. At Conner Prairie Interpretive Park visitors learn how groups of people lived at different times in the same region.

THE ROLE OF STUDENTS AT
CONNER PRAIRIE INTERPRETIVE PARK

Youths apply to Conner Prairie Interpretive Park to be a youth interpreter by filling out a job application anytime between October and January. The job application contains several short-answer essays; the whole form does not exceed four pages on two sheets of paper. Next the youths attend a job interview where they answer several questions from two Conner Prairie Interpretive Park staff members. The panel uses a rating system on the application and on the interview; the panel members take into consideration the developmental differences between ten- and sixteen-year-old youth volunteers.

The youth interpreter's success is based more on ability to be flexible and willingness to try and to learn rather than having a large base of historical knowledge or being gifted in acting ability. Granted, the acting and history skills help, but they are certainly not requirements for selecting new interpreters. Youth volunteers are selected at the end of February. Last year from this pool of applicants sixty-four young people interviewed for twenty positions, and eighty people returned to work for a total of one hundred youth interpreter positions.

Of the ten-, eleven-, and twelve-year-olds there were approximately twenty from each age level represented; for a total of thirty interpreters, approximately fifteen each of the thirteen- and fourteen-year-olds and approximately ten fifteen-year-old or older interpreters. Those youths who were not selected this year were encouraged to reapply next year. Those youth volunteers who returned were already trained, knew what Conner Prairie Interpretive Park was, and knew what their responsibilities on the site entailed. The gender ratio approximates four girls to one boy. The student docents worked a minimum of 120 hours; they did not create discipline difficulties; and they turned in their paper work establishing their work schedule.

Youths must be between ages ten and eighteen to work in this program, but after they reach age sixteen youths may apply to work as part of the Conner Prairie Interpretive Park interpretation staff. Youths view this responsibility as a job, so they get to Conner Prairie Interpretive Park on time and turn in their schedule. If they fail to do either of these tasks, they will not get the opportunity to be hired later. As a result of this policy students call in when they are sick, and they make sure their clothes are clean. They learn interviewing skills and job-application skills as well.

Not everyone is interested in being a youth interpreter, and not all children want to work with the public. One or two students sometimes leave during the first couple of months when they realize this experience is not for them. The largest losses occur from youths moving away from the museum vicinity and at the time students enter high school. At age sixteen, youth volunteers can be employed by Conner Prairie Interpretive Park; thirty-nine former youth volunteers have become paid staff.

Some students who elect not to make the staff commitment become adult volunteers. One youth interpreter could not do the 120 hours or be an employee but wanted to stay connected with the museum. She transcribed an 1880 diary primary-source document as a youth interpreter and later transferred to the adult-volunteer development division. She continued to do research on the document, worked on some special events, joined the dulcimer group, and thus stayed connected. Now she wants to try working again as a first-person adult volunteer.

The youth volunteers do have limits on the site, because safety is very important to the museum staff. The younger students need to tell the director where they can be found, and they need to be under adult supervision. They may not roam the 1,100 acres of the museum. A few of the older youth are not tied to a specific post but are assigned to a historic area. They originate engagement activities and supplement staffing as they see a need in addition to serving as mentors to younger youth volunteers. Procedures are in place to protect the youth volunteers from injury and illness, from training procedures, visitors, weather, livestock, and labor. The intention is to provide a safe environment without smothering the youth interpreter.

FIRST PERSON

Some youths determine that they wish to work only as third-person interpreters while others decide they want to move into a first-person role. The first-person youth volunteers take on a role in the Pioneer Village or on the Victorian Farm. Conner Prairie Interpretive Park historians script these roles for the youth volunteers to the extent that the character and their relations to the family have been written. These are not based on real people, but they are heavily documented historical re-creations by the Conner Prairie Interpretive Park researchers and historians to accurately portray what life would have been like at this time. These are roles that provide realism to the site that cannot be played by adults.

> My favorite person is Sarah Jane McCart because I get to be more outgoing . . . Usually you ask them [visitors] their name and then you ask them where they live . . . and then they ask you the same thing . . . Then you start showing them around your house or you start showing them games . . . Then they go in and you hand it off to somebody else so you can go out again.[2]

Alex explains how she performs her first-person role, how she interacts with visitors, and how she works with other interpreters.

Youth volunteers do not want to make a mistake so they are sometimes hesitant to approach visitors. Often times the adult interpreter will begin speaking with visitors and give a leading question to the youth interpreter that will help them start. Youth volunteers need to work the most on initiating conversations with visitors; they are better at starting chores and games in both first and third person. First person challenges them with picking up period manners and speech. If they are in the same room with an adult interpreter, many times they will let the adult take the lead, but if they are in another room or on the porch the youth can initiate a conversation.

Students usually let the visitor approach them; they are also more comfortable with other children than with adults. If a child approaches them, they respond with, "How are you? Have you ever done this chore before? Would you like to play this game?" Peer to peer the youth are very approachable and usually approach other children more easily than they approach adults. They work especially well with other children who come to visit with their families or with school groups. When the visitors see someone their age playing a game, the youth interpreter provides an opportunity to interact with the visitors.

CHALLENGES FOR THE PROGRAM

If youth volunteers wish to work in first-person areas, they need to bear the cost of their period clothing. That total amount comes to approximately $200 per person per time period, including shoes, socks, cloth, tailoring, and hat, and that assumes that the child does not outgrow the clothing during the year.

Other costs borne by the students include a sack lunch each day when they work and daily transportation to and from the site. Compared to the hefty costs of sports equipment, costs of athletic membership fees, and transportation fees, which include traveling to multiple states for tournaments, this is not a significant amount. The child in a low-income family could still participate in this program in third person and not worry about dressing as a first-person presenter.

Ethnic demographics of the youth volunteers mirror the population of the twenty-first-century suburban county rather than the population of the state in either the 1830s or 1880s. Of the one hundred students, four biracial youth volunteers chose either Anglo Saxon or black American roles; two chose to portray 1836 and the other two elected roles in 1886. The student of Puerto Rican descent and the two children of Middle Eastern descent each play Anglo Saxon characters. While the museum is limited by the ethnicities present at that particular location and time, it has worked diligently to be inclusive in the present.

While youth volunteers do come from forty-six schools and nine counties, geography limits those who can participate at the museum. At some point geography excludes some students because of distance, transportation, finances, time, or a combination of all of these factors. The museum is also limited in how many youth volunteers it can accommodate; presently it can accommodate no more than one hundred youth volunteers. Every year many people contend for a relatively small number of available openings; obviously there is more interest in this program than even this large site can accommodate. It is not known how many students try for multiple years to be a part of this program or if after one rejection they find other outlets for their volunteerism.

With the opening of the Conner Prairie Civil War Journey, additional opportunities for children exist, including students in A Soldier's Aid

Society who are trained in one specialized area and activity for a few specific weekends during the season. Older boys join a Civil War artillery or infantry unit.

WHY MUSEUMS NEED STUDENT PARTICIPATION

The benefits of student interpreters to Conner Prairie Interpretive Park are obvious. They provide realism in the site; no one else can play the role of a ten-year-old as well as a ten-year-old. One hundred youth volunteers contribute over 21,600 hours of volunteer time; this is the equivalent of ten full-time positions. Youth volunteers know the job and are willing to put in the hard work needed to do the job correctly.

After three to five years of free training and a work history that demonstrates dedication, knowledge about Conner Prairie Interpretive Park, and an understanding of what Conner Prairie Interpretive Park expects of them, these volunteers may become employees of Conner Prairie Interpretive Park, as twenty-eight former volunteers have. Some parents of the students become members of the museum while others become adult volunteers. They see the environments in which their children work and realize it is so much fun that they want to do it, too.

WHAT STUDENTS LEARN

In the middle of March youth volunteers participate in the required all-day training prior to actually working on the grounds. This training includes three clusters of information: historical content and skills, procedural and safety information, and interaction with visitors. Youth volunteers are required to attend two additional training sessions of their choice; after that they may volunteer to engage in ongoing training sessions that are held on the same days that they work.

Most youth volunteers elect to go to three or four training events beyond the beginning meeting. They must also do special training to work in special programs. As they gain experiences through the training sessions, they meet criteria that allow them to become certified to do advanced jobs such as building a fire or spinning wool into thread. The agricultural proficiency program pairs the youth volunteers with a member of the staff. As the youth volunteers invest time and experiences in the program they then get different responsibilities culminating in responsible jobs such as driving a team of oxen. Some training sessions are only for the older youth volunteers. Of course, the more experiences they have the more tasks they get to perform.

There are also training opportunities in the form of peer learning and mentoring that occur on the job.

> When I first started I worked in Hands On and there would be older kids out there who had already been working here for a couple of years, and they would teach you what to do. Then with cooking there was a cooking training, and we had lots of trainings for different things. I got my first day in town. Usually they have maybe another kid out there with you helping you, just to help you along . . . The adults are really nice they tell you what to do, and tell you where things are.[3]

Youth volunteers get extensive handbook and paper information produced by Conner Prairie Interpretive Park which instructs them on the work, background, history, programs, roles, interpretation procedures, development of their clothing, and how to care for the historic objects on the site. All youth volunteers meet the standards for interpretation mastery that include: costumer service, professionalism, teamwork, attitude, and meeting goals.

Students are glad to know they are using what they learned in training or from school.

> It gives me another point of view about what I learned in my social studies class, a little bit more of a sense of what they are talking about when they say something that I know I have done. I have a little more sense of what I know and . . . if . . . [my teacher] does not know something that is not in the book she will ask me now.[4]

Some youth volunteers make connections between their school work and their experiences at the museum to make speeches at school, pick literature popular in 1836, make connections to science class, make some of the crafts in the period source called the *Boy's Own Book*, or weave for art-class projects. Youth volunteers become more self-confident when they get to work with many different adults and volunteer in all of the different departments. "When I started working here I would just hide behind my mom, but since I have been working here I have been more outgoing and able to talk to people."[5] Youth volunteers also learn respect and tolerance of the many different visitors with whom they must work as well.

Youth volunteers also have strict guidelines about name tags and appearance that are found in the Youth Interpreter Handbook. Students may not work in first person until they have the clothes for their time period completed and approved by the clothing curator. This gives youth volunteers time to work in third person, to learn background knowledge, and to work with visitors.

The third-person interpreters usually have a post doing a specific program, such as "Sheep to Blanket," where they explain a process or do a craft or activity with a visitor. Youth volunteers are responsible for the activities at special-events programs, and usually there is also a staff person looking after the area. At the Native American Village youth volunteers take responsibility for the hands-on-activities of the day. In the visitors center the students help staff the Discovery Station, a play area for two- to eight-year-olds, Craft Corner, and Science Lab. They meet and greet guests, help guests understand the site, and invite guests to try hands-on activities, which they demonstrate at the site.

Youth volunteers are asked to debrief every day, including what they learned to do that was new to them. They are evaluated with an annual review that involves on-site observation of them at work using a written checklist of expected behaviors, including knowledge of the first-person character and their reaching out to the visitors through engagement theory and appearance. Prior to the annual review meeting the staff member fills out the two-sided form, which was modified from the adult interpreters' form. This instrument in addition to oral feedback provides information for the annual review meeting. In this one-on-one discussion the staff member looks at the progress of the youth interpreter, weighing both strengths and weaknesses in preparation for next year.

Parents may come to this fifteen-minute conference, but usually the staff member conducts these meetings at the end of the season. Youth volunteers are not compared to staff interpreters, but they are expected to perform high-quality work at the teen and preteen level. Some youth volunteers are so well qualified that they could be compared favorably to the staff. After evaluation or training sessions youth volunteers want to improve. They try out procedures and model new behaviors, trying to use the things they have learned.

WHY STUDENTS WANT TO TAKE THESE ROLES

In addition to the evaluation described above, visitors and other staff members use compliment cards to document when they have received exceptional service from a youth interpreter. This relationship is important both to Conner Prairie Interpretive Park and to the youth volunteers. For this program to be successful it must balance accomplishments for both the museum and for the youth volunteers. The youth volunteers are happiest when they know they are making a contribution and when they know their work is valued. At the end of the year both the youth and their parents evaluate the program. Their evaluations include such topics as: What did you think of the year? What did you like? What changes should be made?

Gifted students find that within a secure and supportive community they can use the information that they learn in school. Some students say they cannot learn at school, but they can learn and understand at Conner Prairie Interpretive Park. Other students seem to fit into this museum community although they do not fit in at school. They further state that the museum community is where they learn the most and where they feel the most comfortable.

> A lot of kids will say, "It is just like having another family; they are like my mom or my grandma, or my uncle." They send each other birthday cards; they see each other and give them big hugs in the hall. It is really a very warm and supportive environment. We have a young lady who was having a little trouble in one of her classes at school and one of the interpreters stopped in and said, "How are you doing? Do you need any help?" So it is not just to help you be better interpreters; it is how we can help you be better people.[6]

Students find that they can be smart in this safe and secure environment and that it is okay to have special interests. Talented students do not need to worry about popular opinion. Students muck stalls, spin, and act things out and, here, no one thinks they are weird. Some talented students even begin to think about a future in the museum profession.

While it looks glamorous, the youth volunteers typically work on the site as the children of the family, relative, friends, or hired help to carry wood in for the fire, cook, wash dishes, and sweep. This is all hard work that the youth volunteers are eager to do because when the chores are done they get to play the games of the time. Furthermore, while the adult interpreters must stay at their post in the house, the youth volunteers can move through the village to help bring it to life.

The benefits to youth volunteers are both tangible and intangible. Youth volunteers receive distinctive Conner Prairie Interpretive Park staff shirts for volunteering.

> We want to make sure they feel needed and appreciated. I think the blue shirt is a small way that we can say, "Hey, we think of you just like we think of our staff. We want the visitors to recognize you as an authority that they can come to if they have a question."[7]

Other tangible benefits include: recognition parties, monthly newsletters, admission to programs at which youths volunteer, training sessions, service awards, and a pass for five admissions after completing one hundred hours of volunteer service.

FOUNDATIONS

Students should not have to wait in the wings for some distant time in the future when they will walk upon the stage of citizenship. There are many benefits for students who practice democracy in their schools and communities as part of the formal curriculum and as a part of living in a democracy.[8] A citizen who is well educated through the school, extracurricular events, or the community knows how they relate to one another as citizens.

Citizens use interaction with others to determine their position in the community. Students thrive when they see that they have a place in the community, have opportunities to form connections to their community, and realize that they can help shape their community.

Students who are engaged in service-learning provide a service or product to a real audience while learning academic content and skills followed by structured reflection. While volunteering for community service is prosocial, it is not necessarily connected with academic knowledge, skills, or structured reflection. If students get paid, however, the experience becomes an internship. While service-learning always exists in an educational setting, community service does not need to be connected to education.

Students benefit from service-learning because their learning is set within a community context. The students learn with their peers, but they must also learn with nonchronologically aged peers who are their equals in work but not their age mates.[9] Through working with a community of mentors students get the opportunity to be accepted by adults for what they can do and what they can contribute based on individual merit.[10]

Students find that their learning is neither remote nor abstract, because of the task or situation they are engaged in undertaking. Furthermore, students get to engage in real problems that interest them. Finally, they get to make real contributions that help the community.

Students find ways to supplement social studies understanding when they turn to extracurricular social studies programs and experiences. Students may find extracurricular social studies programs after school through multiple contests. Other cultural institutions such as historical societies, libraries, and museums provide excellent creative extracurricular social studies programs.

Many of these cultural institutions help students make connections through service-learning programs. Service-learning programs have been well defined in education.[11] Service-learning programs help both the students and the institution while securing the student's place securely as a citizen in the community. People who participate in service-learning find academic content to provide the real needs or services of an appreciative audience.

These programs promote democracy and citizenship through social studies education and provide examples of how service-learning can be applied to social studies content in classrooms.[12] Certainly extracurricular service-learning would have many of the same characteristics of service-learning in the school day. Museums that offer service-learning opportunities have heady experiences with content to offer students. Multiple opportunities also exist for students to do service either for the museum or for the visitors to the museum or both. Students, who are empowered to go forward on their own time to provide service to museum visitors, possess the altruism and application of knowledge and skills that would make for excellent citizens of a democracy.

Students have many talents that they have developed over their years in school, at home, or in civic groups.[13] With careful instruction, peer mediation, and mentoring students can hone their skills to such a state that they can act in a professional manner. Students produce a first-person presentation for visitors, peers, and community members.[14] Students can produce high-quality first-person presentations for others when they have learned difficult content and can explain it fluently.

Furthermore, students can produce meaningful reenactments from their experiences and help to create meaning for others. Students can go beyond first-person presentation to recreate an entire mood, day, theme, or event.[15] Reenactments take energy from many people to produce interaction and interpret meaningful community events. A small or a large group may work together to create a small slice of the past that a visitor may experience directly. Direct experience is very important both for keeping the student engaged and for involving the visitor in reenactment events.

CONCLUSIONS

What ideas can interpreters learn from student extracurricular experiences? Interpreters must be proactive in establishing cooperative ventures with local historical museums, sites, and societies. Interpreters need to create extracurricular programs for social studies by working with local historical societies and sites to establish neighboring opportunities for students who interpret local history for their community. Museums have content expertise and resources for social studies enrichment, but most museums do not have education specialists.[16] Interpreters have the educational practice and background needed to make this type of program work.

Furthermore, the advantages to students in acquiring and presenting information are numerous. Youths participate in extracurricular history programs because they are enjoyable and engaging ways to learn.[17] Youths willingly give up time after school, on holidays, and during weekends, because they are excited about what they are doing. Youths make first-person history presentations and re-create events from the past, because it is entertaining, it helps others, and they are good at it. Obviously youths see the importance of volunteering and feel that they have contributions they can make to the community. Furthermore, youths receive positive attention from adults and peers when they are in charge of their post.

Educators usually ignore museums except as destinations for one-stop field trips, but the importance of cultural institutions as societal educators must not be ignored in providing information and experiences to young people. Collaborative partnerships need to be established between more schools and museums in order to provide rich experiences for extracurricular instruction and service-learning. extracurricular programs in museums, historical societies, and libraries can play a pivotal role in creating situations where youths interact with adults. Well-prepared cultural organizations will find themselves advantageously positioned for impassioned students who are hungry for social studies information and experiences.

Cultural institutions support students by providing them with a community where the students can demonstrate their talents. Talented students sort themselves into an extracurricular program at Conner Prairie Interpretive Park. While working with visitors as peers to the interpretative staff, they learn about the past. The youth volunteers enjoy a sense of community where they share a common purpose, feel safe and comfortable, and share responsibilities with their peers.

NOTES

1. Jerry Aldridge, "Teaching to Transform the World," *Childhood Education* 81, 1 (2004): 52–54; Alice W. Terry, "An Early Glimpse: Service Learning from an Adolescent Perspective," *Journal of Secondary Gifted Education* 11, 3 (2000): 115–35.

2. Alex, age eleven, individual interview, June 27, 2004.

3. Meghan, age twelve, individual interview, June 27, 2004.

4. Daniel, age twelve, individual interview, June 27, 2004.

5. Hannah, age fourteen, individual interview, June 27, 2004.

6. A. Barret, individual interview, June 29, 2004.

7. A. Barret, individual interview, June 29, 2004.

8. Carl D. Glickman, "Revolution, Educating, and the Practice of Democracy," *The Educational Forum* 63, 1 (1998): 16–22; Joseph Kahne, Monica Rodriguez, BetsAnn Smith, and Keith Thiede, "Developing Citizens for Democracy? Assess-

ing Opportunities to Learn in Chicago's Social Studies Classrooms," *Theory and Research in Social Education* 28, 3 (2000): 311–38; E. Wayne Ross, "Alienation, Exploitation, and Connected Citizenship," *Theory and Research in Social Education* 28, 3 (2000): 306–10; E. Wayne Ross, "Diverting Democracy: The Curriculum Standards Movement and Social Studies Education," *International Journal of Social Education* 11, 1 (1996): 18–39.

9. Kristen L. McMaster, Douglas Fuchs, and Lynn S. Fuchs, "Research on Peer-Assisted Learning Strategies: The Promise and Limitations of Peer-Mediated Instruction," *Reading and Writing Quarterly* 22, 1 (2006): 5–25.

10. Mary R. Coleman, "Curriculum Differentiation: Sophistication," *Gifted Child Today Magazine* 24, 2 (2001): 24–25; Thomas. P. Hebert and Kristie L. S. Neumeister, "University Mentors in the Elementary Classroom: Supporting the Intellectual, Motivational, and Emotional Needs of High-Ability Students," *Journal for the Education of the Gifted* 24, 2 (2000): 122–48; Sandra Manning, "Young Leaders: Growing through Mentoring," *Gifted Child Today* 28, 1 (2005): 14–20; Ellie Schatz, "Mentors: Matchmaking for Young People," *Journal of Secondary Gifted Education* 11, 2 (2000): 67–87; Kenneth Shore, "Teaching the Gifted Student," *Principal* 79, 4 (2000): 37–39, 42.

11. Rahima C. Wade, "Community Service-Learning: An Overview," in *Community Service-Learning: A Guide to Including Service in the Public School Curriculum*, ed. Rahima C. Wade (Albany: SUNY Press, 1997), 19–34; Rebecca L. Carver, "Theoretical Underpinnings of Service-Learning," *Theory into Practice* 36, 3 (1997): 143–49; Jeff Claus and Curtis Ogden, "Service-Learning for Youth Empowerment and Social Change: An Introduction," in *Service-Learning for Youth Empowerment and Social Change*, ed. Jeff Claus and Curtis Ogden (New York: Peter Lang, 1999), 1–8; Ron Schukar, "Enhancing the Middle School Curriculum through Service-Learning," *Theory into Practice* 36, 3 (1997): 176–83.

12. Richard M. Battistoni, "Service-Learning and Democratic Citizenship," *Theory into Practice* 36, 3 (1997): 150–16; Ronald V. Morris, "Stop Tobacco in Restaurants: Fifth-Grade Students STIR City Hall," *Gifted Child Today* 27, 2 (2004): 22–31; Ronald V. Morris, Service-Learning in a Fifth-Grade Colonial American Unit," *Social Studies and the Young Learner* 15, 4 (2003): 11–14; Rahima C. Wade, "Social Action in the Social Studies: From the Ideal to the Real," *Theory into Practice* 40, 1 (2001): 23–28; Rahima C. Wade and David W. Saxe, "Community Service-Learning in the Social Studies: Historical Roots, Empirical Evidence, Critical Issues," *Theory and Research in Social Education* 24, 4 (1996): 331–59.

13. Paula Olszewski-Kubilius and Seon-Young Lee, "Parent Perceptions of the Effects of the Saturday Enrichment Program on Gifted Students' Talent Development," *Roeper Review* 26, 3 (2004A): 156–65; Paula Olszewski-Kubilius and Seon-Young Lee, "The Role of Participation in In-School and Outside-of-School Activities in the Talent Development of Gifted Students," *Journal of Secondary Gifted Education* 15, 3 (2004B): 107–23.

14. Ronald V. Morris, "Middle School First-Person Presentations and Connection to the Community," *Research in Middle Level Education Online* 26, 1 (2002B): www.nmsa.org/; Ronald V. Morris, "Presidents' Day in Second Grade Using First-Person Historical Presentation," *Gifted Child Today* 25, 4 (2002): 26–29, 64; Ronald V. Morris, "Using First-Person Presentation to Encourage Student Interest

in Social History," *Gifted Child Today* 24, 1 (2001): 46–53; Ronald V. Morris, "The History Walk: Integrated Multi-Age Learning," *Gifted Child Today* 23, 4 (2000): 22–27, 53; Stacy F. Roth, *Past into Present: Effective Techniques for First Person Historical Interpretation* (Chapel Hill: The University of North Carolina Press, 1998); Stephen E. Snow, *Performing the Pilgrims: A Study of Ethnohistorical Role-Playing at Plimouth Plantation* (Jackson: University Press of Mississippi, 1993).

15. Ronald V. Morris, "Experiencing Third Grade at Simmons School," *Social Studies and the Young Learner* 14, 4 (2002): 6–10; David Thelen, "Learning from the Past: Individual Experience and Reenactment," *Indiana Magazine of History* 49, 3 (2003): 155–71.

16. Eric Madero and Marianne Zadra, "Moving beyond the Classroom: Bringing the Past and Future Together for Enrichment Students," *Gifted Child Today Magazine* 24, 2 (2001): 60–64; Mary Witte, "Through Another's Eyes: Engaging Students in Interdisciplinary Curricula," *Gifted Child Today* 27, 2 (2004): 52–53.

17. Ronald V. Morris, "The Clio Club: An Extracurricular Model for Social Studies Enrichment," *Gifted Child Today* 28, 1 (2005): 40–48; Ronald V. Morris, "A Retrospective Examination of the Clio Club: An Elementary Social Studies Enrichment Program Offered as an Extracurricular Activity," *Journal of Social Studies Research* 4, 1 (2000): 4–18; Ronald V. Morris, "The Indiana Junior Historical Society 1960–1970: A Crucible of Democratic Reform," *OAH Magazine of History* 11, 4 (1997): 51–54.

18. Elizabeth Shaunessy, "Questioning Techniques in the Gifted Classroom," *Gifted Child Today* 23, 5 (2000): 14–21.

9

Huddleston Farmhouse 1860 Victorian Life Day Camp

Once each year campers ages nine to fifteen, who are in fourth through eighth grade, meet on Thursday and Friday to learn about the American Civil War through a summer day camp at the Huddleston Farmhouse of Indiana Landmarks on the National Road. On the first two days they convene in the mornings, but on Saturday they open their camp to their families and the public.

On Saturday their parents are invited to join them and even spend the night in Civil War tents, with a departure time on Sunday morning. They learn about early life in America through this extensive experience. The staff and volunteers of Huddleston Farmhouse know they can involve their community and help young people learn history while opening their property to people who would not normally visit this site.

PRACTICAL PROCEDURES

Even though the program exists in a conservative area where stereotypical gender roles are practiced, this feminist program provides young women with activities and experiences that inform them of the ways work, skills, and knowledge was divided across stereotypical gender lines, focusing on the domestic sphere during the Civil War era. Campers learn about life during the time of the Civil War by participating in activities that reflect social history or the daily life activities of the common person. The campers get opportunities to learn about domestic life on the home front by engaging in common activities including cooking, fashion, textiles, clothing, deportment, and dancing (see table 9.1).

Table 9.1: Civil War Day-Camp Schedule

Day	Time	Activity
Thursday	10:00	Still life
	11:00	Candle making
	Noon	Lunch
Friday	10:00	Counted cross-stitch, dish painting
	11:00	Cooking
	Noon	Lunch
Saturday	10:00	Spinning and weaving
	10:30	Fashion Show on the back porch
	Noon	Lunch
	1:30	Adult Civil War primer
	3:30	Ladies' Tea
	4:00	Amherst artillery camp
	7:30	Dance on the grounds

Each day they prepare and cook their lunch over a campfire, and then they clean up after their meal. Each camper learns more about how people lived in the 1860s during the sectional crises of war. This knowledge is compared with life on the home front in the East or the Midwest as experienced by the families and especially children, who were sending their soldiers off to war.

The site of this adventure is Huddleston Farmhouse, an 1840s farm and stop for wagons traveling west on the National Road, which was the first federally funded highway in the United States. The curatorial staff of Indiana Landmarks interprets the site as a transportation museum and, with volunteers, organizes the Civil War event each year.

The event not only helps young people learn about the past but also includes their parents and community members. The multiple-room farmhouse and various outbuildings provide space for rainy days, and the open fields and forest surrounding the house provide a place for work and outdoor activities. While Civil War soldiers might have marched past the site or more likely taken a train past it, the real Civil War camp was the old, county fairgrounds, which is now covered with houses.

The campers, who are completely silent but with the noise of preparations for lunch in the background, use pen and pencil to write answers, telling where they identify products that were invented prior to, during, and after the Civil War. After their predictions, they discuss what they selected. Most of the products are domestic, and campers volunteer stories from the time of their parents rather than the time of the Civil

War. The campers also make connections to grandparents and friends. The docent makes a connection to her mother, and does a good job of explaining the economic connections, the average yearly income, and the cost of various items.

Last year the campers painted china, but this year they work with watercolors to create a still life. The campers receive instruction on the properties of a still life, and they drop the proper lines for horizon and perspective into it. The campers become engrossed in their project, follow the various project steps, and paint the shapes of the solids into their still life. The campers fill in the shapes with light colors first and then the dark ones; they use a paper towel as a blotter. The campers do what well-educated women would be expected to do at this time, but while the campers' conversation strays from the time period, they still work on their project. One of the campers grabs a wooden folk toy as her very sophisticated watercolor still life dries.

The docent gives campers choices about what to do next such as reading a diary or playing games. Campers engage in a spelling bee, play the game of goose, graces, or find a box of toys with which to amuse themselves. Along with a stack of children's books from the 1860s the docent reads a diary to the campers; they are then able to discern the family relations through the primary sources. The docent asks the students to predict what work they could do to help the family. One camper says, "I could take care of the baby, but I might burn the food." They select a favorite quotation from the diary, and they work with pen and ink copying quotations.

After lunch, while campers ate sausage that had been cooked over a wood fire, a docent talks with them about early Victorian foods. One camper knows how sausage is made and another says, "I will never eat sausage again." Soldiers at this time would find food in the smoke house or ripe corn in the garden. It was better to be a soldier in the summer, even though people preserved many types of food for the winter and early spring.

Preserving food required salt for pickling or packing food in lard. Because of the use of salt for preserving, there were many types of pickles and many types of ketchup, which was used interchangeably for sauce. Civil War soldiers and families would have depended on these stored foods to help them survive the winter.

The campers make a Sunday doll from a handkerchief. One girl asks, "Did she give you directions?" The docent said, "No, so we will just figure it out." The campers become silent for this activity, and they start with a cotton ball head and a ribbon around the neck. They knot the corners for hands and add a stitch for the eyes on the face. They add lace around the bottom edge and successfully figure out how to construct the doll. This is one of the few craft-type activities in the day-camp program, but it is very appropriate to the time period that they discussed. The campers work with looms weaving cloth tape and using wood cards. Many different activities are available so the campers can go from one activity to the next.

The campers dress in early Victorian fashion and style their hair appropriately for the period; they dress as children dressed in the 1860s for formal occasions. First they try on stockings and the elastic tube garters to hold them up, and then they make the connection to the diary entry which they have read about darning socks. Next the girls, in rapid succession, put on their pantaloons, chemise, corset, corset cover, petty skirt, hoop, hoop skirts, and dress and take on the appearance of Victorian lassies.

The girls compare the hoops to the clothing of today, talk about the types of dresses, and examine the buttons. The docent says, "They come right out of shells." Camper: "Is that why they bend?" Campers button their shoes and then try sitting in hoops before putting on their hats. They compare themselves to the china head dolls of the time. Finally, the girls take pictures of themselves in the formal parlor of the Huddleston Farmhouse while they have a fashion show and a tea party. During these activities the campers enjoy talking about what they did last year at this camp.

First they talk about good posture and walking straight, and then they talk about positions to avoid such as never crossing one's knees. They make connections to ideas they have heard in other places and what they hear in the present. The campers also make the connection to hoops being conducive to airflow; the girls then sway in their hoops to move the air around. They consider heat stroke and learn where ice can be secured to keep cool. Campers make the connection that hose both then and now are hot, but they do not need to worry today about cracking a rib when they cough while wearing a corset. The docent and the campers agree that they feel different when wearing period clothing.

After first putting aside their hat and fans, the campers learn to dance in their long, historical dresses. First they walk through the movements of the dance without the music. Next they learn about their dance card and the social implications connected with it. The card has room for eight dances on the front and eight dances on the back of it. Of course, they learn to curtsey before going to the barn to learn the Virginia Reel or the Gay Gordon. While dressed in period clothing the campers learn about gender roles during the 1860s, and they talk about the expectations for children at that time. Campers can rattle off the expectations of women as a wife; because the campers have lived with these same expectations in their small towns and communities, they are very familiar with them.

Each transition allows a choice of activities, and the campers determine to find out about the reenactor's camp area. They learn about tent cities near the soldier camps, and they visit the tent area of the reenactors to discover the equipment in use there. The campers examine and compare a variety of the things they saw to those that campers today would take with them. From the chamber pot to the triangle, washboard, and clothes-pins the campers look at the differences in a wheelbarrow and the fabric combinations of a morning dress (what the campers would call a house-coat). With this information the campers realize that the camping these people did was in high style and not at all like what their peers talk about when they determine to go camping. The people in the 1860s camped because they were refugees or were following the movements of an army.

CIVIL WAR EXAMPLE

Many populations interacted in this day camp. The role of parents and community members allowed them to come for the day, enjoy the festivi-ties, and spend the night with their child in a recreation of a Civil War tent. Jim Orr, then in charge of programs for the Huddleston Farmhouse, organized a team of volunteers to work with the campers. This prominent group included an elementary-school teacher and a retiree who is now a full time reenactor; they spent the most time with the students.

The volunteer museum educator worked with food service, and the Huddleston Farmhouse grounds keeper worked with site preparation. Many other volunteers including a southern soldier, the Lincoln inter-preter, the men of the U.S. 19th Infantry, and the U.S. Colored Troops' chaplin interpreter all worked with students during the course of the day camp. Most of these volunteers dressed in period clothing, and two of them made presentations in the first person. These well-prepared vol-unteers always had a backup plan and options if the original program did not work.

POSSIBLE PROBLEMS

There are a couple of areas that the personnel involved with the program might wish to reconsider. The small number of campers in this group at times seemed problematic. Just a few more campers could have sustained more discussion; with the small number of campers the docent had to work hard to keep the campers engaged. More than once the campers lapsed into silence. More campers in the program could help the social interactions of those who participated and might help to spur additional questions. Everyone involved with the program would welcome more campers to the program.

Concurrent with the small number of campers, it is hard to keep the interest of campers with low-energy activities. All of the activities, while absolutely historically authentic, were too passive for a long-term exposure. Children in 1860 and the twenty-first century need a variety of experiences with high adventure and vigorous energy expenditures. The dancing was a great example of a high-energy activity, but the period clothing of the time discouraged the expenditure of energy and encouraged docile and passive behavior. Unlike the 1860s when girls were conditioned for domestic lives, girls of the twenty-first century enter civic life as equal players.

ANOTHER EXAMPLE

In a contrasting example, a group of twenty students did a Civil War reenactment one weekend with the purpose that they would live for one twenty-four-hour period in a particular period of time (see table 9.2). They created a story that explained their gathering at one spot (see table 9.3) before engaging in a variety of experiences that would expose them to daily life activities (see table 9.4). The site of the reenactment was a log cabin and the events took place on the grounds. Students examined social history

Table 9.2: Permission Slip

Dear Parents:
The Clio Club will present a Civil War reenactment on Friday and Saturday, April 12 and 13, 20XX. Each student must dress for the weather in addition to wearing cotton or wool clothes. Because of fire and spark danger, synthetics are highly discouraged. Student may arrive at 5:30 p.m. and depart at 6:15 p.m. The students will need a $10.00 nonrefundable deposit, sleeping bag, and pillow.

Sincerely,

Dr. Ronald V. Morris
Manager of the
Clio Club
---(clip here)---

My child, _____, may participate in the Civil War reenactment.

_____

parent's signature

PLEASE RETURN THIS FORM WITH THE NONREFUNDABLE DEPOSIT TO DR. RONALD V. MORRIS BY MARCH 29, 20XX.

Table 9.3:   Reenactment Story

In 1862 the southern army was heading south on the road from Pleasant Hill to Harrodsburg, Kentucky. The Union Army was rapidly closing in on the force. The Union Army, encamped in the woods, included enlisted men, towns people who discussed the events of the day, and people who supported the army, but nearby the enemy was on patrol . . . .

Table 9.4:   Civil War Reenactment

Day	Time	Event	Activity
Friday	5:30 p.m.	Recruitment Center	
	6:30 p.m.	Billy Yank	
	7:30 p.m.	Mr. Lincoln	
	8:30 p.m.	Civil War through song	
	10:00 p.m.	Lights out/picket duty	
Saturday	6:00 a.m.	Wake up/fix breakfast	A. Crullers
			B. Potato cakes
			C. Toast
			D. Milk/butter/honey
			E. French toast
	7:00 a.m.	Eat breakfast	
	7:30 a.m.	Abolitionist minister	
	8:00 a.m.	Session I	A. Union infantry display
		[30-minute rotation]	B. Marching
			C. Artillery training
	9:30 a.m.	Artillery firing	
	10:00 a.m.	Mrs. Lincoln	
	10:30 a.m.	Restroom break	
	10:40 a.m.	Mrs. Wallace	
	11:10 a.m.	Session II	A. Homemade sausage with sage
		[30-minute rotation]	B. Baking powder biscuits/corn fritters
			C. Annie's baked corn/vegetable soup
			D. Applesauce
			E. Oatmeal cookies/green beans
	1:40 p.m.	Lunch	
	2:10 p.m.	Abolitionist's wife	
	2:45 p.m.	Session III	A. Roll cartridges
		[30-minute rotation]	B. Rifle firing
			C. Clothes repair
			D. Salt pork
			E. Hardtack
	5:15 p.m.	Shaker	
	5:45 p.m.	Debriefing/conclusions	
	6:15 p.m.	Depart	

through the daily life experiences of the people they met. The students also learned from reenactors, guest speakers, and first-person interpreters about the perspectives of the people whom they met at the reenactment.

The first thing that happened to the students was that they joined the Union Army with the requisite paperwork. The students arranged themselves in the log cabin for the night and by firelight and candlelight the students met a soldier back from the war, who told about his life in the Union army and his experiences in the war.

The students also met a man who was a friend of Mr. Lincoln; he described the president including a lot of material from primary sources. The students sang Civil War songs around the fire before taking their turn at guard duty. They gave the sign and countersign on their watch until they were relieved by the next group of sentries who protected the camp all night. Students learned about the life of a Civil War soldier by recreating the events of joining the Union army.

The next day the students cooked both their breakfast and lunch over open fires. Breakfast included crullers, potato cakes, toast, milk, freshly churned butter, honey, and French toast. For lunch the students made homemade sausage with sage, baking powder biscuits, corn fritters, Annie's Baked Corn, vegetable soup, applesauce, oatmeal cookies, and green beans. Students learned how much of their time was absorbed by cooking and cleaning in addition to comparing food of that period with food of today. In the twenty-first century students worked together in groups to prepare their meals; they discovered that they are very far removed from where their food originates.

In the morning all of the students learned to be soldiers. They learned about the infantry and how to march in formation, how to drill, and how the artillery worked by loading and firing a cannon. In the afternoon they learned about the work women and men would do in factories to prepare supplies for the Union army. They rolled cartridges, repaired clothing, packed salt pork, and baked hard tack for the front. Students performed all of these jobs to replicate the tasks and skills of the people from the past.

During the day the students met a variety of people who came past their camp and paid their respects while visiting the troops. These people all spoke through first-person presentations. They met an abolitionist minister, who wanted to reform society by purging the country of slavery. The role of women figured prominently in the events of the day. Mrs. Lincoln came past to cheer the troops, and she talked about the Lincoln family and the political issues of the time. An abolitionist's wife who was active on the Underground Railroad talked with the students about directing slaves to the North. Mrs. Wallace also came past on her way to visit with her husband, General Lew Wallace. Since she was well educated, articulate, and accomplished, she talked about women's reform movements.

A female Shaker came from just down the road at Pleasant Hill, Kentucky to visit with the students. As a person who opposed war she offered hospitality to people from both the North and the South, to slaves or to those who were free. The day ended with the students reviewing the people they had met and the ideas they had encountered; moreover, the students evaluated the work of women and men in the army or on the home front. In this example students worked with many ideas about what life was like during the Civil War and the multiple perspectives expressed through meeting a variety of people.

REENACTMENT CONNECTIONS

Many educators use experiences and a variety of texts to help elementary-school-age students understand the social studies content about the Civil War. Information books, historical fiction, and narrative texts all set the stage for students to create their own characters and plot. Teachers help structure student experiences through the use of advanced organizers and help the students to interact with narrative by encouraging them to create their own narrative.[1]

The information the students have prior to reading helps them determine which information is most important and how it relates to other information; furthermore, this information helps the students as they interpret the narrative to create their own text using the same events. Moreover, teachers use primary sources with their students so that students use actual data from history to determine the events without interpretation from others. Students engage in question generation as they work with a primary source across time.[2] Students who use these documents find comparisons between figures in the past and their present experience.

Students can also use technology to acquire Civil War primary sources such as census data from Web sites. These primary sources allow the students to examine the life of real people in the nineteenth century, particularly the perspective of ideology in motivating people to fight for a cause.[3] The soldier's daily life and tragedies suffered by families on the home front illustrated people who lived and died for their beliefs. The perspectives of these people and the perspectives acquired by the students about the people of the Civil War are of significant interest to some educators. Schillinger (2007); Caine, Caine, and McClintic (2002); and Wasta and Lott (2000) all use language arts skills to develop students' perspective.[4]

By promoting the mastery of the subject, encouraging imagination, developing effective questioning, and using creative materials, teachers endeavor to develop a learning community that helps students form an emotional connection to the people and events under study. A variety of source materials including primary sources, which are sometimes accessible through Web sites, allows students to form perspectives about the real people who lived in the field or on the home front at the time of the Civil War. Teachers help students develop perspectives about the Civil War through a variety of experiences.

Students take content knowledge and apply it in other types of experiences, such as reenactments. Reenactment experiences help students look at other sources of information to help them find themselves in history immersion experiences. Students experience the lives of people in minority populations through reenactments of the Trail of Tears, New France, and Ellis Island Immigrants.[5]

The experience of these people in uncomfortable situations from the past contrasts with the very comfortable life experiences of many of the student participants. These experiences resulted in direct student engagement with problem-solving and social studies research experiences. Students worked with mentors, peers, and first-person presentations to learn about differing perspectives of people from the past.

Many historical societies, museums, and cultural institutions have experimented with a variety of formats and model summer-camp experiences to provide early encounters with history content. Summer programming allows students in rural, suburban, and urban settings access to needed knowledge and skills. While all children are heavily taxed by standardized tests in schools, some children have more access to outdoor experiences and camps while other students are confined to screen-based activities, which limits social and emotional growth.[6]

When students develop their emotional and social skills through camp-type programs, they learn about living and making ethical choices. Cultural institutions facilitate this type of ethical experience when they provide camp-type programs. The students involved with these programs find opportunities for making positive choices.

Feminist scholars try to discern how best to educate young women to prepare them to succeed in the world. Young women need relationships to construct self-esteem during adolescence. There is a linear increase in the number of young women between eighth and twelfth grades who develop relationship authenticity and self esteem.[7] These findings support the authors' views that the feminist development framework links understanding and explanation of female adolescents. Feminist scholars have also looked at the role of single-gender learning experiences in promoting positive growth for girls.

When fourth- through eighth-grade students experienced optional single-gender classrooms, younger students preferred the experience more than the older students.[8] Academic success, especially in math and science, seemed promising for girls; while boys reported more bullying, girls reported more overt interpersonal aggression. For cognitive development, single-gender academic classes for girls seem to offer potential for attainment of knowledge and skills as well as gains in both self-esteem and relationships. Feminist educators look at both the effect of the instructional setting and the content when determining an appropriate curriculum for girls.

In textbooks authors tend to ignore, marginalize, or exclude women's history, thus giving the appearance that women did not take part in significant major events of national and world events. Including the voices and roles of women and minority women in the elementary-level social studies curriculum is imperative for citizens in a diverse democracy. Teachers can weave women back into the elementary-level social studies curriculum when they examine their own past, use oral history interviews, and consult primary sources.[9] Each of these authors looks to resources beyond the standard elementary-school textbook for ways to connect students into the history of their community.

Other authors mention specific strategies for teaching women's history and including it in the curriculum. To develop an understanding of women's history, students use primary sources, drama, dispel stereotypes, and include architecture.[10]

Each of these strategies holds the potential for examining gender relationships in a democratic society. Both the exclusion and the inclusion of women history in the curriculum informs boys and girls about the nature of power held by gender groups across the past and into the present. One-half of the students in our classes are waiting to find out how their gender fit into the past and how it fits into the present.

CONCLUSIONS

The American Civil War is a popular topic that entices students to learn about a segment of American history. A variety of people in the community are also interested in this topic, and they work with historical institutions to convey content. Staff members at cultural institutions help students, their parents, and the general public learn more about this period of time. Groups of boys and girls learn about life during the Civil War when they participate in re-created events exploring that time period. Direct experiences help students understand this hard and non-glamorous life.

Reenactment programs provide in-depth immersive experiences for students, giving them real-life adventures that they could not get from just reading a book or watching a media screen. The experiential learning engages all of the senses and helps students to examine the effort it takes to live in a different time and place without the conveniences of the twenty-first century. The reenactment also provides a social and emotional connection to people from the past. As young persons, students learn how adults define their life with conventions, manners, and education. For casual children of the twenty-first century, the ideas of play and work in the formal Victorian Era were very different from today.

The summer-camp format allows students to experiment with content and a period of time without a long-term commitment to the activity. The students get to do some sampling of the offerings of the cultural institution. The staff members of museums offer high-interest and high-engagement programs to students during nonschool hours to attract attention to the mission of the cultural organization. Students get to go to Civil War camp to explore special topics that may have implications for developing interests that they will further explore as either a vocation or an avocation. The camp format allows students to both learn and find felicitous amusement during their nonschool hours.

Using a feminist lens, girls learn about the role of women on the home front during the American Civil War. They engage in specific experiences common to women in the 1860s. They learn in a gender-specific class that looks at culture, history, geography, and economics, as well as at individuals, groups, and institutions. The all-girl classes allow for an environment in which the girls do not need to worry about asking questions in front of their male peers. Furthermore, the girls develop peer relationships and self esteem in mono-gendered groups.

Women's history helps children of both genders understand the contributions all members of society make to the creation of the world in which they live today. The Civil War camp helped girls to see and experience the role of women in the history of the 1860s. The girls learned many aspects about women in the Civil War from refugees to camp followers at the front or behind the lines at home. The girls felt how constrained and confined they were by clothing that was designed to keep them passive. The girls saw their contributions in the reenactment and the contributions of women in the curriculum of the camp activities.

Indiana Landmarks does an outstanding job in planning a children's program and making it a family and then a community program. By deliberately offering programming in which children and parents experience activities together, not only do children and parents learn together, but they also have common experiences that they discuss at the present time as well as in the future.

The Saturday programming is designed for parents to experience the time with their children while cooking dinner or sleeping under the stars; moreover, the community is invited to experience the event also; the community is specifically invited to a Civil War dance on Saturday evening. Indiana Landmarks not only meets its goals for programming for children, but it meets its mission by getting new people from the community and new visitors to visit the site and learn about historic preservation.

NOTES

1. Nancy W. Fordham, Debra Wellman, and Alexa Sandmann, "Taming the Text: Engaging and Supporting Students in Social Studies Readings," *Social Studies* 93, 4 (2002): 149–58.

2. Eula W. Fresch, "Connecting Children with Children in History Using Primary Sources," *Southern Social Studies Journal* 27, 1 (2001): 38–49; Ronald V. Morris, "Use Primary Sources to Develop a Soap Opera: As the Civil War Turns," *Social Studies* 93, 2 (2002): 53–56.

3. Haydee M. Rodriguez, Cinthia Salinas, and Steve Guberman, "Creating Opportunities for Historical Thinking with Bilingual Students," *Social Studies and the Young Learner* 18, 2 (2005): 9–13.

4. Geoffrey Caine, Renate N. Caine, and Carol McClintic, "Guiding the Innate Constructivist," *Educational Leadership* 60, 1 (2002): 70–73; Trace Schillinger, "Humanities and the Social Studies: Studying the Civil War through the Third Space," *Social Education* 71, 7 (2007): 384–88; Stephanie Wasta and Carolyn Lott, "Civil War Stories: An Integrative Approach to Developing Perspective," *Social Studies* 91, 2 (2000): 62–68.

5. Daniel A. Kelin, II, "To Feel the Fear of It: Engaging Young People in Social Education," *Talking Points* 14, 1 (2002): 10–14; Ronald V. Morris, "How Teachers Can Conduct Historical Reenactments in Their Own Schools," *Childhood Education* 77, 4 (2001): 196–203.

6. Dorothy T. Damore, "Preschool and School-Age Activities: Comparison of Urban and Suburban Populations," *Journal of Community Health* 27, 3 (2002): 203–11; Ginny Deerin, "Giving Youth the Social and Emotional Skills to Succeed," *New Directions for Youth Development* 108 (2005): 117–25.

7. Emily A. Impett, Lynn Sorsoli, Deborah Schooler, James M. Henson, and Deborah L. Tolman, "Girls' Relationship Authenticity and Self-Esteem across Adolescence," *Developmental Psychology* 44, 3 (2008): 722–33.

8. Dale Baker, "Good Intentions: An Experiment in Middle School Single-Sex Science and Mathematics Classrooms with High Minority Enrollment," *Journal of Women and Minorities in Science and Engineering* 8, 1 (2002): 1–23; Benjamin K. Barton and Robert Cohen, "Classroom Gender Composition and Children's Peer Relations," *Child Study Journal* 34, 1 (2004): 29–45; Frances R. Spielhagen, "How Tweens View Single-Sex Classes," *Educational Leadership* 63, 7 (2006): 68–69, 71–72.

9. M. Gail Hickey and Don L. Kolterman, "Special Women in My Life: Strategies for Writing Women into the Social Studies Curriculum," *Social Education* 70, 4 (2006): 190–96; Carol C. Warren, "Viewing American History through Native Eyes: Ideas for Sharing a Different Perspective," *Social Studies and the Young*

Learner 18, 4 (2006): 15–18; Jill Weisner, "Awakening Teacher Voice and Student Voice: The Development of a Feminist Pedagogy," *Feminist Teacher: A Journal of the Practices, Theories, and Scholarship of Feminist Teaching* 15, 1 (2004): 34–47.

10. Mary E. Connor, "Revolutionary Women: Portraits of Life in the Thirteen Colonies," *Social Education* 64, 1 (2000): 12–15; Sharon M. Fennessey, *History in the Spotlight: Creative Drama and Theatre Practices for the Social Studies Classroom* (Westport, CT: Heinemann, 2000); Joanne K. Guilfoil, "From the Ground Up: Art in American Built Environment Education," *Art Education* 53, 4 (2000): 6–12; Andrea S. Libresco, "History Mystery: A Documents-Based Lesson on Women's Rights," *Social Studies and the Young Learner* 13, 2 (2000): 1–4; Teresa M. McCormick, "Fear, Panic, and Injustice: Executive Order 9066—A Lesson for Grades 4–6," *Social Education* 72, 5 (2008): 268–71; Jonathan Miller-Lane, "Constructive Disagreement, the Body, and Education for Democracy," *Social Studies* 97, 1 (2006): 16–20.

10

Integrating Music and Social Studies in an Extracurricular Activity

The Voyageur Ancient Fife and Drum Corps

The Battle of Mississinewa 1812 is a remembrance of Native People and noncombatants caught in continent-wide conflict during the War of 1812. The soldiers massacred the occupants of the village in the attack, and this event has become an annual reenactment and community remembrance. Many students visit this reenactment to learn about the War of 1812 and the western frontier.

INTRODUCTION

Students from age eight to eighteen grab their fife and drum, dress in their period clothing, and present a musical show from the colonial period. They meet every Monday to rehearse for one-and-one-half hours; once a month they perform at an event; and two or three times a month they participate in a parade. They work after school and on weekends to present historically authentic musical programs as part of their extracurricular group, the Voyageur Ancient Fife and Drum Corps. Students stay in the group because they form a vibrant community of peers that travels and performs together. They share common experiences and common interests in a mutually supportive and collaborative environment.

These students participate in an extracurricular activity that allows them to integrate social studies content and music. They practice for the purpose of demonstrating their proficiency in a public performance; an event may involve the entire weekend or only one hour for a parade. They are not attempting to replicate a particular person, group, or event, and their commitment to gender equity would have been unthinkable in the

137

1700s. The members of the group attempt to keep history alive by recreating life, not just military history, in the time period that would have had fife and drum members from age eight to fifteen.

This is not a military group; they neither march with weapons nor fire guns, but they do perform at many events that also contain those elements. They represent an interest in heritage conservation by interpreting and representing one of the different groups of people that came into the area in the 1700s. They do stand for an idea of authentic historic music performed before thousands of people every year by young people using period instruments. The children preserve a folk music tradition of musical exchange between groups.

CARROTS AND (DRUM) STICKS

Due to the maximum age qualification, the corps is ever changing and the membership requirements evolve with the needs of the group. The Voyageur Ancient Fife and Drum Corps accepts all students, but criteria are set and students meet specific expectations. The drummers come from the fifers within the group. Students must learn five songs before they can travel to events, and they need to learn ten songs to get a uniform and march with the group. In celebration they earn a real rosewood fife in a ceremony for having learned the first and second groups of fifteen songs. The members of the group do not stop with just fifteen songs in their musical repertoire, however.

There is a positive response for each achievement in learning to march or perform the music, and the hardest part seems to be getting over fifteen songs memorized. The director needs to help them get over this point so they do not get stuck there; after getting over this mental plateau they take off memorizing tunes with seeming ease. If a child becomes frustrated in getting to the first fifteen songs, the child typically steps back and returns later; the parents give the child space and allow the child to drop out for a period of time. After students learn fifteen songs on a plastic fife the group bestows on them either a B-flat fife of secondary quality or rosewood drumsticks to the drummers. Even though the second-quality fife has small flaws in the wood, it not only sounds better than the plastic one, it is easier to play.

When a fife player learns thirty-five songs, a landmark has been reached and the group buys the player a very fine rosewood fife; snare drummers earn a strap and a second set of drumsticks to wear, and bass drummers receive rosewood beaters and a leather holder. The group members believe that they are making investments in one another when each student progresses at their own rate. By the time students learn thirty-five songs they are hooked on participating in the program. The students have proven that they can meet the standards of the group and can perform for audiences. They are on their way to becoming ideal members of the group.

The ideal corps member attends events and group rehearsals, practices individually every day, is serious about this commitment, and is dedicated to the corps. Students must maintain a 70 percent or better attendance record to remain a member of the group; illness, family illness, and school events are all excused. Students practice once a week except following a performance. In evening rehearsals they march and perform in the parking lot of a local elementary school, and when the sun sets they go inside and practice by sections. When they practice, they rarely look at the music, and they always perform without music.

As a junior corps they do not need to be as strict in the music they select as an adult corps. The students play authentic period music from the French and British colonial experience as well as Scottish music. Some events require music performed only from a certain time period while other events are out of their time period so students learn music of other eras, too.

If younger players do not know a piece they stand ready to play until a piece is selected that they can perform. Older students select the set and usually perform period music first followed by music for the specific event, and finally they select inclusive music that all of the students can play. At most events, in the last musical performance at the end of the day all musical groups on the site play the same songs in one great finale.

COMMUNITY

Each fife and drum corps selects a theme for use in designing their uniforms. When the Voyageurs formed in 1969, they elected to look like the founders of their community. French voyagers came from Canada to trade and set up a trading post called Post Ouiatanon, which later became Lafayette and was located among the Wea Indians on the banks of the Ouabache, or Wabash River. The authentic period clothing that this group models is that of the French Canadian voyagers with moccasins, leggings, tan knee breeches, colored shirt, sash, head scarf, and stocking caps.

When wearing this period clothing, the group looks like a horde of young people who engaged in the fur trade and made music on the frontier of New France. Even though the corps members all dress in a similar fashion, it is a series of common events and experiences that draw them together.

At practices the students start to build community, but it is really the events that make people feel like a family. This happens almost immediately; when they are away from their parents for twenty-four hours, they consider each other an extended family. Corps members do not camp, but they do spend prolonged periods of time living and working together. When they go to events they spend the night in churches, YMCAs, school gyms, or other places that are free; they provide their own sleeping bags and air mattresses. YMCA facilities are a favorite place to stay because they have a pool, but corps members also bring Nerf footballs and card games for amusement.

The corps members do work on the trips, bring items to share, or do specific tasks to help the group. In their community they must take responsibility for the group packing and unpacking, they have obligations to help the group move equipment, and they take the initiative to help the group set up in order to perform. The social aspects of friendships within the group are important, but so is the common goal of performance.

ADULT ROLE

The group is incorporated through a board of directors that includes the volunteer director, and parents who serve as president, business manager, treasurer, and fundraiser. The board also has two corps member representatives and two community member representatives. The parents elect their members who volunteer to serve and the corps members elect their representatives as described in their bylaws. Decisions are made based on majority votes of the board. The board acts to make sure corps members are safe and supported.

The board watches over the group to make sure that all of the children have a good experience and get along with one another. Members of the board have written standards of behavior for children and parents so there is no question as to what is expected. The board members want control, but they do not wish to restrict the children; the board members want the participants to grow as individuals from the experience. The leaders want the students to react to the experience and be able to perform. In addition to making sure the students are safe the board makes sure the students are supported and have the resources that they need to continue to perform.

Once each year at the Feast of the Hunter's Moon the board sponsors a vending booth because they are one of the host corps, but they do not do this anyplace else. They do very little fundraising because children who are eight years old cannot do it and high-school students have schedules that are hard to work around. The corps members rely on earning fees from participating in parades and events, and parents donate gas money. They have also recently received their first grant from the Tippecanoe Arts Federation.

Their entire fundraising is needed to ensure that there is support to keep the program going for the next generation of corps members.

The present director served as a volunteer until appointed by the board twenty years ago; he serves without pay at the pleasure of the board. The director of the group keeps a record of attendance. The director looks for and determines individuals who can teach their peers and who have the character and abilities to work with other people at different levels. Then the director finds corps members who want to do that, and they give them opportunities to do it. The director looks for and documents peer-tutoring skills so that when students go to college and they need letters of recommendation, the director has plenty of evidence of leadership experiences.

The only two paid employees of the group are the fife and drum instructors. They are hired by the board and paid for each rehearsal, but it is not a princely sum. Instructors work with students who need extra help prior to practice and work with small groups of students during the practice session. The corps board members continually work to have people in line who can and will work with young people. Much of the adult leadership comes from the parents of the corps members.

Families support the students by driving them to events and practices. Interested families support student learning; when the parents talk with the children about history children become immersed in it. The interest that parents model is patterned for the students. The corps styles itself as a family group and involved parents form friendships when they travel to different events with their children. The parents seem to enjoy the opportunities the group provides as much as the corps members themselves do.

Parents find many benefits when their children participate in the corps. The parents say that they enjoy meeting interesting people with the group; they like to travel and say they have always had a love of history. They also say that they get to do things they would not normally do as well as have fun and do things as a family regardless of their children's age or gender. One set of parents has two boys and two girls the same age in their family, so the entire family goes together with dad and mom. The multiage and dual-gender group is not like organized sports where the children all go indifferent directions. Another one of the benefits for these families is that at high-school graduation there is a scholarship for those children who have stayed in the group.

PROBLEMS

A good event is one that produces income for the group, is enjoyable, close, and historically accurate. A bad event is the negative of one or more of the above situations; occasionally an event will promise to pay the group but does not come through. This is about the worst thing that can happen though. Corps members must make a limited financial commitment to the group by providing their own moccasins, original fife, and spending money for trips. The individual corps members have a small investment in the group compared to the resources spent on them by the group.

Another potential problem is that outdoor performances are only fair weather events and once the weather gets cold the events cease until spring. There are not many indoor performance venues for fife and drum corps. They do not perform in the month of December except for the local Christmas parades and to escort Santa into the Mall. They practice patiently until spring so when communities need parade or festival participants, they will be ready.

By the end of an event everyone in the group is tired. It can be physically taxing to march in a long parade across rocks or asphalt in moccasins. The weather may be hot or cold for their festival, thus draining them of energy. They are all tired from the emotional energy of being around people, exerting emotional energy by performing, and becoming physically tired from traveling together. Fortunately, the musicians are young and energetic and bounce back quickly.

The extracurricular social studies experiences are not automatic, systematic, standardized, nor easy to assess. The social studies learning varies from year to year or from event to event. For the students learning occurs as a result of their group experiences, preparation, travels, performances, and the events they attend. For example, they learn national anthems for flag-raising ceremonies at the different events where they perform. They learn about ethnic groups, regions, and nations by performing their music. They may pick up information from the events where they participate and carry that into individual research.

In another example, a child did an article on Charbonneau because she learned about him from a reenactment, became interested, and investigated him further. Unlike a school curriculum, extracurricular activities have no formal assessments for social studies, no scope and sequence, nor is there a book of standards. It is easy to observe that the students could be watching TV or playing video games, but instead they have chosen to perform music in historical clothing. Spending all of that time going to historical sites and associating with historical reenactors provides them with a set of experiences completely foreign to many students.

CORPS MEMBERS

Of the twenty members of the group, ten are male and ten are female, though it has varied from three boys and nine girls to eight boys and five girls. Families tend to be involved, including one family with four members, a family with three members, and two families with two members presently in the group. In addition to working with sibling relations, different ages are included; of the twenty members, thirteen are thirteen years of age and younger with a majority of corps members being ten years old. Based in Lafayette, Indiana, the group of students primarily works with students in the county, but members do come from a five-county radius. They work well together.

There is no competition in the group. It is a positive environment, not a popularity contest, with everyone being equal in the group. The students do not have to compete with anyone but himself or herself, and there are no losers. The more songs students learn, the more they can do, and the more they can play. The more they play the more they teach their peers.

The key to peer tutoring is to find those corps members who want to bring other members up to their level by teaching them and working with them. They are the ones other corps members emulate and admire. This is hard to do, so it takes experimentation as one older child is paired with one to three younger students. They use informal and fluid ability groups to help students learn to play the next song or group of songs.

After a while it becomes obvious either through observation or self-evaluation who can and who cannot teach the younger students. Sometimes students actually learn faster from their peers than from the fife or drum instructors. Former corps members also continue to make contributions to the group when they periodically come back for three to four consecutive weeks to practice with the present corps.

In order to recruit new corps members the current members go to elementary schools and play in talent shows. Students have a variety of reasons for being in the group, but most of the participants are originally invited by their friends or families in their elementary-school years. They talk about it, their friends know how they spend their time, and their friends come and watch. They brag to all their friends that they are staying at the local historical festival called the Feast of the Hunter's Moon. Students stay with it because of the friends they make and the places they get to go across the United States and Canada.

After many years of saving and raising funds the corps members finally took their first ten-day summer tour. The corps performed in a huge parade at Deep River, Connecticut, for the Muster of Fife and Drum Corps with corps from all over the country. The Voyageurs corps members were in awe of these groups. Most of the groups were adults, including the Old Guard, some were family corps with parents and children in the same group, and some were youth corps, but none of them were as young as the Voyageurs Ancient Fife and Drum Corps.

The corps members visited the whaling community of Mystic Seaport. They had first-time experiences when they tried lobster at a restaurant overlooking the ocean, and they swam in the Atlantic. They spent a day in Boston before visiting Fort Ticonderoga, Crown Point, Fort Niagara, and Niagara Falls. Their last stop was a performance for the Drums along the Maumee event at Ft. Meigs in Ohio.

Students experience education through formal and informal methods; most of the events have a set time for them to perform for formal education. The newest members of the group are excited about being included in the group, and they wear their uniforms to school for presentations to show people what they are doing. The corps members perform at the Feast of the Hunter's Moon Education Day. They do the entire program where they explain about their clothing, history, and instruments, demonstrate how their instruments work, and tell how they perform their programs.

In the education program they demonstrate how their instruments work, but they do not do a musical show; they talk about the corps and historical events. Students learn the purpose for the clothing and tell about what they wear. At that event they plan and carry out the presentation on their own, and they urge students to come and join them because of their great experiences with their friends and the historical sites they get to visit. Informally children and adults also approach them and ask them questions about their clothing and music. The corps members usually work person to person when a member of the audience asks the students what they are doing.

The corps members see the group as rewarding. It is a group with a reputation; they are well known in the eastern United States and Canada with a tremendous reputation for marching and both quality and volume of sound. The students know that if they join they will be part of a significant group with a good reputation. They are always recognized by the members of the crowd at regional events such as the Battle of Mississinewa near Marion, Indiana, and the Johnny Apple Seed Festival in Fort Wayne, Indiana. The corps members realize that adult groups such as the Court Recorders Convention in Chicago call them and invite their group to come and perform.

FOUNDATIONS

Some students show gifts in learning social studies and talents by performing music, and these talents may be in just one domain or they may cross over into multiple domains. Students gifted in social studies may need the provided experiences in citizenship education. Talented students need civics and problem-solving experiences in their social studies curriculum since they live in a democracy.[1] Their social studies curriculum needs to be of sufficient challenge to maintain their interest.[2] At the same time, talented musicians attribute their success to multiple factors.

Students talented in music attribute their abilities to hard work, but the home environment is also important for talent development.[3] When education and instruction assist in its development, musical talent may be encouraged by study that combines two or more disciplines. Some students get integrated study in music and social studies. School curricula that provides coordinated and systematic study about both music and social studies should exist for students; students enjoy this combination of integration.[4]

The musically talented people who brought their musical heritage to North America also heard music from other people who brought their music with them. Through the use of music to illustrate the culturally diverse musical traditions that intersected in America, students discover multiple musical traditions that are still present.[5] Countless musical exchanges from other places and tunes were exchanged between people.

Most of the time students learn social studies through the school curriculum, but occasionally they learn social studies through extracurricular activities. Teachers have the opportunity through both the social studies curriculum and through extracurricular activities to encourage civics and citizenship skills.[6] Students develop their social studies talents by going into depth through extracurricular activities.[7] An informal exchange of knowledge or folk tradition has been a vibrant learning environment for people across time.

In a folk tradition people fluidly pass songs from teacher to learner back and forth, switching roles multiple times—now the learner, next the teacher. Folk traditions usually depend upon peer teaching to sustain a community with a common pool of knowledge. Usually a folk tradition exists in a community where people have power, because they demonstrate their prowess by authentic performances.

Students learn and work in communities, especially when they are working together in musical performance. Students work in communities to make contributions and solve problems and to listen to one another.[8] Within those communities the students exercise power. Adults can help students to exercise power in managing student affairs and in student acquisition of knowledge, skills, and values.[9] One of the ways students exercise power in their community is through peer tutoring. As an authority they are able to convey knowledge to others who are a very real audience.

Many different groups of students engage in peer tutoring where they are effective in accomplishing tasks. Students engaged in peer tutoring have improved their acquisition of social studies knowledge while reducing their off-task behavior.[10] In addition to peer tutoring the community members engage in authentic assessment when students perform before an audience and are judged by the members of the greater community. Students use authentic assessments in social studies to make contributions to the community beyond the classroom.[11]

Students who engage in authentic learning move their learning beyond the classroom and into the world. Student learning needs to focus on a real problem, provide a real solution or action, and it needs to be addressed to a real audience. Students give authentic performances when they perform music before groups of people.

CONCLUSIONS

Clearly these students are talented and committed. They have multiple experiences where they jump into the middle of major historical events and community celebrations. While learning social studies is not the most important aspect to the students, it is obvious that the students are much more aware of regional historical events than are their peers.

While they focus on performing they have obviously traveled to many more sites than their peers have while living in a close and supportive community of their own construction. These students are engaged in authentic performances of excellence two or three times a month when visitors cheer them, applaud their skills and talents, and local celebration committees pay them to come to their festivals, reenactments, and events.

Teachers who teach gifted and talented students should take note of this group. Here is a group of students who are musically gifted and who create performances under very authentic circumstances before crowds of adults who most likely paid a gate fee to get to hear the group. They look and sound like an authentic group of early musicians. The students accomplish their achievements through an informal grouping system, featuring peer tutoring and noncompetitive experiences. Furthermore, they work with adults and their parents in mutually supportive endeavors at an age when many students are in physically different activities from their families.

For practitioners of social studies there are several items to note from this group. First, the students establish a close community that exists across multiple years and is founded on collaboration rather than competition. Second, they self-select into a group that values the re-creation of historically musical performances, and they give large chunks of time to associate with community-based historical events. Finally, even though they do not get the most sophisticated historical understandings that could come from excellent instructional practice, the participants come away from their extracurricular experiences with deeper understandings than that of their peers who do not engage in such free-time experiences. Members of the field of social studies could only hope that more such extracurricular experiences were available to students and students would take advantage of them.

NOTES

1. Don Ambrose, "Aspiration Growth, Talent Development, and Self-Fulfillment in a Context of Democratic Erosion," *Roeper Review* 28, 1 (2005): 11–19; Felicia A. Dixon, Kimberly A. Prater, Heidi M. Vine, Mary J. Wark, Tasha Williams, Tim Hanchon, and Carolyn Shobe, "Teaching to Their Thinking: A Strategy to Meet the Critical-Thinking Needs of Gifted Students," *Journal for the Education of the Gifted* 28, 4 (2004): 56–76.

2. Ronald V. Morris, "The Indiana Junior Historical Society, 1960–1970," *Organization of American History Magazine of History* 11, 4 (1997): 61–54.

3. Robert J. Evans, Robert Bickel, and Edwina D. Pendarvis, "Musical Talent: Innate or Acquired? Perceptions of Students, Parents, and Teachers," *Gifted Child Quarterly* 44, (2) (2000): 80–90; Joan Freeman, "Children's Talent in Fine Art and Music—England," *Roeper Review* 22, 2 (2000): 98–101; Joanne Haroutounian, "Delights and Dilemmas of the Musically Talented Teenager," *Journal of Secondary Gifted Education* 12, 1 (2000): 3–16.

4. Melissa R. Bulls and Tracy L. Riley, "Weaving Qualitatively Differentiated Units with the World Wide Web," *Gifted Child Today Magazine* 20, 1 (1997): 20–27, 50; Mary F. Erler, "Exploring World Cultures with Music," *Social Studies and the Young Learner* 17, 1 (2004): 30–32.

5. Renard B. Harris, "Middle Schoolers and the Blues," *Social Studies* 95, 5 (2004): 197–200; Adam F. Rosenbloom, "High School Music Studies and Social Studies: An Interdisciplinary Approach," *Music Educators Journal* 90, 3 (2004): 41–45.

6. Michele Schweisfurth, "Education for Global Citizenship: Teacher Agency and Curricular Structure in Ontario Schools," *Educational Review* 58, 1 (2006): 41–50.

7. Ronald V. Morris, "The Clio Club: An Extracurricular Model for Elementary Social Studies Enrichment," *Gifted Child Today* 28, 1 (2005): 40–48.

8. Theodoric Manley, Jr., Avery S. Buffa, Caleb Dube, and Lauren Reed, "Putting the Learning in Service Learning: From Soup Kitchen Models to the Black Metropolis Model," *Education and Urban Society* 38, 2 (2006): 115–41; Michele Schweisfurth, "Education for Global Citizenship: Teacher Agency and Curricular Structure in Ontario Schools," *Educational Review* 58, 1 (2006): 41–50.

9. Anand R. Marri, "Building a Framework for Classroom-Based Multicultural Democratic Education: Learning from Three Skilled Teachers," *Teachers College Record* 107, 5 (2005): 1036–59; Cheri F. Triplett and Anne Hunter, "Talking Circle: Creating Community in Our Elementary Classrooms," *Social Studies and the Young Learner* 18, 2 (2005): 4–8.

10. Mariette DeHaan and Ed Elbers, "Peer Tutoring in a Multiethnic Classroom in the Netherlands: A Multiperspective Analysis of Diversity," *Comparative Educa-*

tion Review 49, 3 (2005): 365–88; Ya-yu Lo and Gwendolyn Cartledge, "Total Class Peer Tutoring and Interdependent Group-Oriented Contingency: Improving the Academic and Task-Related Behaviors of Fourth-Grade Urban Students," *Education and Treatment of Children,* 27, 3 (2004): 235–62; Vicky G. Spencer, Thomas E. Scruggs, and Margo A. Mastropieri, "Content Area Learning in Middle School Social Studies Classrooms and Students with Emotional or Behavioral Disorders: A Comparison of Strategies," *Behavioral Disorders* 28, 2 (2003): 77–93.

11. Patricia G. Avery, "Authentic Assessment and Instruction," *Social Education* 63, 6 (1999): 368–73; Patricia G. Avery, Dana Carmichael-Tanaka, Jennifer Kunze, and Nonie P. Kouneski, "Writing about Immigration: Authentic Assessment for US History Students," *Social Education* 64, 6 (2000): 372–75; Jere Brophy and Janet Alleman, "Assessment in a Social Constructivist Classroom," *Social Education* 62, 1 (1998): 32–34.

11

Conclusions

Students thrive on direct experiences when they engage in historical reenactments, and they also get a better understanding of daily
life through their interactions with the past. Thus the principles of the
reenactment experience incorporate intellectual, social, and emotional
aspects. Reenactors find satisfaction when they engage in three types of
experience including civic, deliberative, and hands-on activities to make
meaning of their event. The environment they help create surrounds them
with experiences that stimulate their senses. Students integrate multiple
skills and experiences into the event.

Reenactments, through hands-on experiences, help students become
more responsible for their own learning. They also talk to one another
about the events of the time, and they enact these experiences. Playfully
engaging with one another for a sustained interval allows for interaction with other reenactors to enjoy the group experience. Students have
direct experience with these ideas as they experience and live with them
during historical reenactments. Because reenactment is predicated on
experience, students learn from studying the events in a fashion similar
to doing ethnography.

Powerful key ideas for teaching social studies are learned through reenactments using ethnographic methods in the classroom. Teachers develop
deep understandings and undertake rich experiences when they engage
in historical reenactment as lived experience. Historical reenactment provides students with an opportunity for gathering the data of lived experience as in ethnography. The reenactment helps students to use drama in
learning both empathy and critical thinking, and student ethnographers

research and live in the culture. Historical reenactment presents an opportunity to work with knowledge of the most social worth to highlight important concepts and ideas.

Reenactment experiences provide in-depth immersive types of experiences to students, thus providing them with lived adventures they could not get from just reading a book or watching a media screen. The experiential learning engaging all of the senses helps students to examine the effort it takes to live in a different time and place without the conveniences of the twenty-first century. These direct experiences help students understand how hard and nonglamorous this type of life was. Students make a number of choices prior to engaging in events, and students must think on their feet as the day unfolds. Groups of boys and girls learn about life when they participate in re-created events and explore a specific period of time.

INQUIRY

Inquiry requires students to raise questions, use logical reasoning, and conduct research. Social studies educators need to promote inquiry to encourage students to hold problems as their own. Students experience history rather than just passively receive it when they are involved in inquiry-based projects. Historical reenactment depends upon the process of inquiry to guide the exploration and investigation of events and situations imposed by the conditions of the reenactment. The intellectual aspects of reenactment include power, curiosity, and educative function.

The students have a great deal of autonomy and responsibility for their learning in the reenactment. Perhaps the developmentally appropriate nature of students who are ready to cut more strings from parents and adults would make this type of autonomous learning more appealing for older rather than younger students. Older students certainly are ready to strike out in small groups in order to investigate. While it is important to give students opportunities to explore history in depth, future study should concentrate on both the quality and quantity of information the students gather from this experience. Teachers give the students opportunities to explore when students get to compare their present to the past; students focus on those things from long ago and far away as being ripe for inquiry and wonder.

Students make choices about what they learn from a reenactment experience while they gather information and conduct research to bring back to their classroom. The environment of a reenactment requires students to raise questions about what they are seeing, use logical reasoning to determine conclusions, and conduct research on the site to gather information. The participants need the power to shape their own questions, and the reenactment experience needs to incite curiosity and ignite the desire to explore more. The students connect their prior knowledge with new learning. When students work in small groups, the members of their peer group modify their research project as they plan and attend an event.

In their groups students must raise questions about the sites they are seeing, use logical reasoning to determine if their plan is working, and conduct research about how their group is working. In reenactments students need suggestions and limits set by teachers on where to go, what to do, and how to do it. They apply a critical lens to the reenactment in order to evaluate what they are seeing and experiencing.

Students work with cultural universals to spark questions, engage in decision making, and participate in civic engagement. Culture universals are big ideas that students use to talk about multiple groups of people across time or space when engaged in historical reenactment. Students use cultural universals when they participate in programs designed to learn about shelter, clothing, and food. Students use peer teaching when they provide instruction to their age-mates, who come to work with them in creative programs when they learn about food traditions, construction details, and clothing traditions. After reviewing cultural universals, which were the ideas first discussed in social studies at the primary level, students get real-life experiences when they work together in community to experience historical reenactment.

PERSISTENT ISSUES

Teachers use reenactment to encourage historical thinking and substantive learning about topics under study in social studies class. When teachers take the time to plan and conduct a reenactment, they bring students off the sidelines and into the heart of discussions and conversations. By giving students some latitude in selecting an assignment that motivates them, teachers encourage decision-making skills through this event.

Students learn about these events and find how different people see these same events through multiple perspectives. Students abate egocentrism and ethnocentrism while examining multiple perspectives when they engage in role-taking during reenactment. The students make decisions in work groups and examine past decisions made by others.

COMMUNITY

Students engage in community events to discover a sense of place, and to find that their community had a role in the past. Many unique events occur in the students' own community, whether it is defined as a state, county, or village. Communities still have reenactment events, and students get to attend these where they witness the interaction of individuals with their peers.

Students engage in multiple examples of community celebration that tie them to immediate people, events, and places. Students witness and participate as community members when they replay former events and create new traditions. A community celebration includes multiple activities that promote the multiple perspectives, groups, and cultures represented in the community. Through reenactments, students connect with their community in order to understand what happened in it and how it operated over two centuries ago.

Students find out about their community through experiences that allow them to relive events. Students use reenactment experiences and events from their community's past to learn how people lived and related to one another. Students develop their class community by engaging in common events and sharing experiences that allow them to explore the past.

The thoughts and dreams of educators move into other aspects of building a community when schools are a place where community development occurs. The school as an intellectual institution provides leaders and talent for community-based solution seeking. Involving people from both within and outside the school through reenactment helps define the community and the relationship the student has to it.

Community members find opportunities to volunteer and a place for intellectual enrichment through reenactments. Students meet with members of the community, who plant the seeds for service-learning activities. Students have common experiences, discussions, and activities that build connections with people in addition to their peers.

Students recognize community issues and seek solutions to redress those problems through direct action. Student solution seeking is the first step in community problem solving and civic efficacy, and students learn about history by experiencing a small segment of it in great detail through reenactment. Students develop historical empathy when they work in community in literacy or speaking and listening experiences. The students find the content relevant because the pioneers come to look more like a modern community with a mix of people who did not always get along with one another.

The school reenactment allows the family to share their history as a recognized part of a national story. Students take this time to acknowledge the connection between their family history and the larger context of history. They particularly find out about the past from one another through opportunities to talk about their family history and traditions. The family members compare their experiences to the circumstances that other people faced. Thus students learn history that applies to their lives; they also learn about the people who live in their town, who are sometimes even their relatives. Students see their younger and older siblings and even their teacher learning with them during the reenactment.

Students, parents, and grandparents engage in intergenerational learning during reenactments. Schools are a place where families learn together, and they learn from one another about different people, places, and times. Whole families learn that school is a place where everyone regardless of age gains knowledge. Students model learning from their parents and grandparents; they in turn model learning for their younger siblings.

By deliberately offering programming that children and parents experience together, not only do children and parents learn together, but they also have common experiences that they talk about both at the time and in the future. The programming is designed for parents to experience the time with their children while engaged in common activities; moreover, the community is invited to experience the event. A reenactment rejects an individual experience in favor of a significant common experience with a family or group. Furthermore, students work with adults and parents in mutually supportive endeavors at an age when many students are involved in physically different activities from their families. Reenactment does an outstanding job in taking a children's program and making it a family program and finally a community program.

The learning environment provided by peer tutoring allows students to demonstrate depth of learning when they engage in historical reenactment. The students remain on-task and provide thoughtful interaction when they engage in peer teaching. The students' discourse in peer teaching allows them to learn more when they engage in historical reenactments.

The reenactment provides a social and emotional connection to people from the past. The reenactment has a definite social component, because people share common experiences, ideas, and values when they invest time in each other. There is intergroup interaction, and of course the element of play needs to be present so that the event is felicitous. The reenactment satisfies an emotional requirement, and regardless of their age the reenactors access the event at their own emotional level. The emotional satisfaction of reenacting keeps reenactors returning to similar events across multiple years.

MENTORS

Students work side by side with adults to accomplish a common task when students work with mentors. Students enjoy working with adults, and the low adult-to-child ratio allows the adults time to listen to the students. Students learn to solve problems in democracy when they work with mentors, and mentors provide role models for demonstrating civic competency. Mentors play a key role in working with students during historic reenactments; many of the guests perform in the first person by telling a historical narrative. Mentors help students learn knowledge, skills, values, and attributes when they participate in historical reenactments. The mentors help students find common concerns within society that they then work to redress.

COLLABORATION

The students establish a close community that exists across multiple years, founded on collaboration rather than competition. Students who collaborate take what they learned in preparation from the classroom and connect it to what they learn at a reenactment. The students accomplish their achievements through an informal grouping system, which features peer tutoring and noncompetitive experiences.

Students not only enjoy the process of reenactment, but they also learn social studies content and skills including compromise. While at a reenactment, students use democratic problem-solving skills to negotiate organizing and carrying out a plan that requires compromise; that in turn allows all members of the group to feel good. By working in a group and staying in a group on a festival site, students practice finding common ground for solving problems through negotiation, compromising, and reaching consensus.

If the reenactment were completely free play, reenactors would just go to the pool or the playground rather than to a museum, a historical society, or a living history site. The reenactment must have some sort of educational function. Educators usually ignore cultural institutions except as destinations for one-stop field trips, but the importance of museums as societal educators must not be ignored in providing information and experiences to young people. More collaborative partnerships need to be established between schools and cultural institutions in order to provide rich experiences for extracurricular instruction or service-learning. Teachers and students find content and situations for historical reenactment provided by the interaction of several elements, including cultural institutions.

Cultural institutions support students by providing them with a community where the students demonstrate their talents. Well-prepared cultural organizations will find themselves advantageously positioned for impassioned students who are hungry for social studies information and experiences. Museums have content expertise and resources for social studies enrichment, but most museums do not have education specialists. Reenactments not only meet goals for programming for children, but they meet institutional missions by getting new people from the community to visit sites such as museums, historical societies, or living history centers.

Interpreters must be proactive in establishing cooperative ventures with local historical museums, sites, and societies. Interpreters want to expose students to history at an early age so that students have an adequate context for understanding. Interpreters in reenactments form a community of interest in this topic, and they work with historical institutions to convey content. Interpreters have the educational practice and background needed to make this type of program work. Staff members at cultural institutions help students, their parents, and the general public learn more about this period of time.

The students get to do some sampling of the offerings of the cultural institution. The students enjoy a sense of community where they share a common purpose, feel safe and comfortable, and share responsibilities with their peers. While working with visitors as peers to the interpretative staff, they learn about the past. Furthermore, students receive positive attention from adults and peers when they are in charge of their post. The reenactment of an individual, group, or hobby helps students have a variety of experiences that serve to enrich their lives.

EXTRACURRICULAR ACTIVITY

Youths contribute to reenactments as extracurricular activity and re-create events from the past because it is entertaining, it helps others, and they are good at it. Youths participate in extracurricular history programs because they are enjoyable and engaging ways to learn. Extracurricular programs in museums, historical societies, and libraries play a pivotal role in creating situations in which youths interact with adults. Talented students sort themselves into an extracurricular program at cultural institutions. Finally, the participants come away from their extracurricular experiences with deeper understandings than that of their peers who do not engage in such free-time experiences.

Interpreters create extracurricular programs for social studies by working with local historical societies and sites to establish neighboring opportunities for students who interpret local history for their community. The staff members of museums offer high-interest and high-engagement programs to students during nonschool hours to attract attention to the mission of the cultural organization. Youths willingly give up time after school, on holidays, and during weekends because they are excited about what they are doing. Members of the field of social studies could only hope that more such extracurricular experiences were available to students and students would take advantage of them. A reenactment is a popular event that entices students to learn about a segment of American history.

The reenactment summer-camp format allows students to experiment with content and a period of time without a long-term commitment to the activity. Students get to go to theme camp to explore special topics that may have implications for developing interests they further explore as either an avocation or a vocation. The camp format allows students to both learn and find felicitous amusement during their nonschool hours.

STUDENT COMMITMENT

Obviously, youth see the importance of volunteering and feel that they have contributions to make to the community. Clearly these students are talented and committed to reenactment. They self-select into a group that values the re-creation of community based historical events, and they give large chunks of time to associate with it. They have multiple experiences in which they jump into the middle of major historical events and community celebrations. Students travel to many more reenactment sites than do their peers while living and working in a close and supportive community of their own construction. It is obvious that these students are much more aware of regional historical events than are their peers.

FINAL THOUGHTS

Student participation in the reenactment instruction occurs primarily in three durations; in the first duration the reformed school day allows a reenactment for a period or a section of the regular school day. The school schedule modifies spatial needs, aides, tutors, lunch, and special classes to accommodate the activity. In the second duration, the whole day includes a typical school day with either an extension in the morning or after school to allow people extra time for activities. Students experience the reenactment through resource people, special events, and time on-task. The final duration, which is a twenty-four-hour day, gives the students time to feel the connections between sunlight and the work day.

History and drama work together to provide the content for the historical reenactment, which is both open ended and interactive. Student reactions to reenactments are very favorable. Children understand the contributions members of society make to the creation of the world where they live today. Students experience the centrality of a fire for heat and cooking as well as truly feeling the drudgery of carrying water and chopping wood to cook every meal. Students produce products, ideas, beliefs, and they garner a tremendous feeling of personal accomplishment when they finish their task satisfactorily.

About the Author

Ronald Vaughan Morris is a professor in the Department of History at Ball State University where he teaches graduate and undergraduate students. He earned a PhD in social studies curriculum and instruction from Purdue University, an MS in educational psychology and gifted education from Purdue University, and a BS in elementary and middle school education from the University of Indianapolis. He taught fourth-grade social studies for eight years and has taught elementary social studies in Purdue's Gifted Education Resource Institute for fifteen years.

Morris is the coauthor of *50 Social Studies Strategies for K–8 Classrooms* (2010) and the author of three books: *Bringing History to Life: First-Person Presentations in Elementary and Middle School Social Studies* (2009); *Drama in Elementary and Middle School Social Studies* (2010); and *The Field Trip Book: Study Travel Experience in Social Studies* (2010). Additionally, Morris has produced seven DVDs for elementary-school social studies classroom use and has even won one Emmy Award. Likewise, he has coproduced a computer game to teach Civil War content to elementary-school students. "Morgan's Raid" was named the Outstanding Project of 2011 by the Indiana Historical Society.

In 1998, Morris won the National Council for the Social Studies Christa McAuliffe Award and, in 2010, he earned the American Association of State and Local History Award of Merit for a life time of service to public history. Presently, Morris is restoring an 1830s row house when he is not hiking on the Appalachian Trail.

CPSIA information can be obtained at www.ICGtesting.com
Printed in the USA
BVOW021509280212

283949BV00003B/1/P